DENNY SEIWELL

The Best and Worst of Times

by Denny Seiwell
& Robyn Flans

Edited by Joe Bergamini

Produced by Rob Wallis

Book and Cover Design by Michael Hoff

Cover photo courtesy of Jess Ferrara Photography

Back cover photo courtesy of Alex Solca

HUDSON MUSIC®

CONTENTS

At Rick Allen's Raven Drum Foundation event to benefit first responders in Palm Springs, CA, circa 2023. (Photo by Monique Seiwell)

FOREWORD

I met Denny in 1968. I was playing with Gabor Szabo at the time, and he was playing in a killer band with Joe Beck, Roger Kellaway, Tom Scott and Chuck Domanico. They loved playing odd meters and they were great at it. It was obvious that Denny was an amazingly talented drummer, but what struck me most was his overall musicality.

We always enjoyed talking about our parallel paths and how at about the same time around '70 or '71, both our lives were changed forever by our associations with the Beatles guys. Denny with McCartney was a great combination. Paul needed somebody to play with great feeling, but also someone who could play odd bars and things. "Live and Let Die" alone tells you almost everything you need to know about Denny's playing.

But in these last few years I've really begun to appreciate his dedication to helping others with and through his own recovery and how he gives back. I know what he does in that world, and it flabbergasts me. He's such a giver and it's so impressive to me; that's the essence of goodness. We talk a lot about that these days, and mostly I tell him how glad I am that he's in my life.

Jim Keltner

PREFACE

The book you are about to read is a collection of the memories of my life. They may not be the way each and every person involved remembers them, but I believe this account to be completely accurate.

This is more than a book about a drummer; it's a human story. I wanted not only to chronicle my life as a musician, but also to share my personal journey, including the ups and downs of a marriage that has survived for 58 years through the darkest period of my addiction.

My story includes success in an impossible business, reaching heights with artists with whom I could only dream to associate. But it also covers the profound effect substance abuse had on my life and those around me and how recovery changed my life. It truly has been a life packed with incredible highs and lows, full of the BEST AND WORST OF TIMES.

Denny Seiwell, March 2025

THANK YOU'S

My wife, Monique, my soulmate, my rock, my partner, my everything.

My father Don Seiwell, who gave me his love for playing drums.

My mother Fay Seiwell, who supported me from being the worst student to the best musician in the school. She always supported me in whatever I did.

My late brother Darryl, who carried the torch of music in our family. I am so proud of him and his family.

My sister Paula and her family.

My late brother-in-law Maurice Noyer and his kids Nicolas and Chloe, whose art and love of jazz inspired me.

My men's group "The Lifeboat," my brothers in recovery. Without their example, I'd be lost.

Professor Charles Fronheiser in my hometown, who nurtured my musical life and gave me opportunities to learn.

Mr. Roy Knapp in Chicago, who was my teacher and mentor.

Chuck Domanico, my best friend, who, without his cheerleading and recommendations, I never would have worked in this town.

James Newton Howard for having faith in me to play on some of his largest orchestral film scores.

Steve Porcaro for being my brother in so many ways and inspiring me musically and spiritually.

A special thank you to Joe Porcaro and Emil Richards.

All the great drummers I listen to and have gotten inspired by, especially Elvin Jones and Mel Lewis. Jeff Porcaro was in a class of his own, as well as my dear friends Jim Keltner and Steve Gadd.

A huge thank you to Scott Redman, Steve Abrams and all my brothers in recovery who walked this path with me.

Dave Black for giving me the opportunity to write my only drum book *What Not to Play! A Drummer's Guide to Crafting a Drum Part*.

Rob Wallis for giving me the opportunity of a lifetime to create this book.

My co-writer Robyn Flans who "gets me" and had the patience and understanding to get the best from me.

My dear friend Joe Bergamini for making a drummer that flunked the 11th grade sound somewhat intelligent.

Backstage at Dodger Stadium, 2014. (Photo by Monique Seiwell)

THE MOMENT LIFE CHANGED

A 27-year-old Denny Seiwell, who was making his bones as a New York session drummer, walked onto the dirt floor of the dingy basement room of a brownstone on West 43rd St. To his complete surprise, in the corner of the near-empty space sat one folding chair with both Paul and Linda McCartney sitting in it together. The year was 1970, New York City.

"You're Paul McCartney," Seiwell stated.

"That's me," McCartney replied. "We're in town and we want to do a record, and we wanted to look at some drummers. Would you mind playing for us?"

"Of course not," Seiwell said, looking at the ratty set of red drums from Studio Instrument Rentals that sat in the middle of the floor. "Do you have a bass or guitar so we can play together?"

McCartney said, "Nah, just you."

Seiwell thinks the following quip got him the gig: "Well, I guess if you can't get it on by yourself, how are you going to get it on with somebody else?"

That broke the ice when McCartney laughed. Denny asked if he would mind if he set up his toms and McCartney told him to go right ahead.

So, Denny put up two tom toms and commenced to take direction from McCartney: "How about playing some rock 'n' roll time?"

Seiwell thought, "I know what this guy wants; he's looking for Ringo." So, he went straight for his toms: boom blat, boom blat.

"He loved it," Seiwell recalls. "He had a big smile on his face. Then he said, 'How about playing a shuffle?'"

Seiwell did. Then McCartney asked him to play a half dozen different grooves, and Denny kept it fun.

"In the back of my mind I thought, 'If Paul McCartney is in New York, looking to make a record I have a snowball's chance in hell of getting this gig.

There are so many great drummers in this city that he's gotta be seeing them too, so I just gotta figure this is the only day I'm going to get to hang out with Paul McCartney. It's only the three of us in the room, so just have fun.'"

McCartney thanked him and Seiwell left, thinking he'd just met a Beatle and if nothing else, he'd have a story to tell for the rest of his life.

And here is that story…

Don and Faye Seiwell circa 1942. (Courtesy Seiwell family archive)

MY BEGINNINGS

Denny admits growing up in the small town of Lehighton, Pennsylvania he was a "jazz snob" with lots of big band records playing in the Seiwell home. Some of that music included Tommy and Jimmy Dorsey, from Lansford, another small town in Pennsylvania, not far from Lehighton.

He describes Lehighton as a real slice of Americana: a mile square—1st Street through 10th Street—with 7,000 people

His dad, Donald Seiwell, was a weekend warrior drummer, playing clubs and along with the Men's Concert Band, while holding down a job at the Packerton Shops as an airbrake repairman on the trains, one of Lehighton's prime industries. Denny was the firstborn of three children

The area is steeped in culture with Native American history including the Gnadenhutten Massacre where Pennsylvania militiamen slaughtered some 90 unarmed Native Americans. Seiwell says there he was always aware of the large memorial to the Native Americans in the local cemetery.

"As a kid we would play at all the cemeteries on Memorial Day and I remember reading that plaque," Seiwell recalls.

As a young boy, Denny and his friends would often find Indian arrowheads as they played in the woods.

The Lehigh River provided much industrialism and the Lehigh Valley Railroad furnished a great many jobs for years.

A lot of the Seiwell's life centered around the Zion Evangelical United Church of Christ. His mom, Fay, was the church secretary, his father was a deacon, his grandfather was an elder, his sister, brother and grandmother sang in the church choir and Denny, who boasts 13 years of perfect attendance in Sunday School, passed around the collection plate. Denny's first dances were in his church, too.

He remembers the bells in the steeple that rang out the time were given to the church by Magina Mantz, the woman who took care of his mother. "Her husband traveled the world on ships and she lived next to us in a mansion on 1st Street. She raised my mother because both her parents were working folks and just couldn't afford to, so Magina raised her and gave her all the best things. They were the first people in my hometown to have an automobile."

Denny had seen his dad playing drums and he wanted to do that. "We didn't have a TV until I was about three," Seiwell recalls. "But they used to set me on the floor of the living room when we got a TV with a pair of drumsticks, and I would drum on the floor and when they would pick me up at the end of the night to put me to bed there would be a hole in the rug."

The family's musical roots went back a long way. Denny's grandfather's brother, Ronald "Bunny" Snyder, was a trumpet player who left Lehighton and traveled the world with acts like Milton Berle in the '40s and '50s. He lived in New York and Miami and was such a colorful figure that he made the gossip columns, seen on the arm of many a popular singer.

Bunny would come up to Pennsylvania for the weekend and stay with the Seiwells, who would let the kids stay up late to listen to Bunny's road stories. Later on, he became a Union representative.

"That was better than Christmas for me," Denny remembers. "He had guns and weapons, too. He would come up to my hometown and he would buy a weapon at the local barber shop because he became a police detective in New York (before he was a union rep)—not one for real, but an auxilliary detective who was allowed to have one—and he'd show us a gun once in a while or the Blackjack he'd carry. Uncle Bunny was it!"

Denny's grandfather's other brother Numa played the violin and was the music director at East Stroudsburg University. "He was really well known in the local area and wrote charts for big bands. He had two sisters, Ruthie and Gicker, who had a singing group with my mother that sang with the local bands. There was always music around the house. Even at family picnics there was music. There were the fireman's picnics, too, where the bands would come from all over the little towns around and they would have a big parade and the firemen would have a beer garden at the end of it. I think that's where I had my first beer, probably at 13."

Don Seiwell behind Denny's first post-Navy kit, playing at grandparents 50th anniversary party, circa 1967.

It was music, music, music, and growing up with his father going out to play music every weekend, that was where the spark ignited.

"When I was 3 years old I was taken up to the Flagstaff Inn in Jim Thorpe, where my dad was playing. I sat on the stage next to where my pop was playing, and that's what lit my fire, I'm pretty sure." Originally called Mauch Chunk, the town of Jim Thorpe was renamed in 1954 for the Native American Olympic gold medalist. Thorpe had never set foot in the town during his life, but the town acquired his remains and set up a memorial to him after his death. It was just a couple towns away from where Denny grew up.

Fast forward a few years and sometimes his dad would leave his drums set up in the front room. When he would leave the house, Denny would jump on the drums and start playing. When his father would get home, he'd yell at him, "Get off my drums!"—in a loving way, of course.

At age 13, Seiwell had a little rock 'n' roll band from Jim Thorpe. He can't recall how that came about, but both other band members, Jack Utsick (with whom he connected later in life) and Bobby Pantella, lived there. They didn't play any gigs or anything, but somehow or another, one of their fathers arranged for them to audition to play on Ted Mack's *Original Amateur Hour*.

"And we got on the show!" Denny exclaims. "We wore little red and black outfits with a bow tie. There was a girl who lived in Jim Thorpe who owned a radio station in Nanticoke, Pennsylvania (up near Scranton), and she had the capability to make a direct-to-disc recording. We went up there and recorded this song we learned called 'Slow Walk,' and we got on the show."

When Denny was 14, a group of parents took a bunch of the local kids to Philadelphia to dance on *American Bandstand*. It was one of the girl's birthdays, so she was picked to dance in the spotlight; when she got to choose a partner, she chose Denny. Seiwell says he always won dance contests because he was "full of fun."

Full of music and full of mischief, too.

"I remember once when I was around 16 and my brother would have been 11 or 12, we played a concert in the bandshell of the park," Seiwell recalls, describing it as a "mini-Hollywood Bowl." "It had really good acoustics and in the percussion section that day was my father, my kid brother Darryl, me and my uncle Eddie, who was playing the bass drum."

Darryl passed away in June 2024, but Denny remembers so many good times with his baby brother.

"I tortured him when we were kids. We slept in bunk beds, and I would sing, 'Happy trails to you until we meet once more,' and he'd get so mad at me. I would spit on him from the upper bunk, little spits," Denny says with a little laugh.

Seiwell says Darryl had to endure living in his big brother's shadow for his whole life, as people would ask him, "How's your brother Denny doing?"

But of the three siblings, Darryl was the only one who went to college, where he studied music. Denny tried to talk him into being a session player because "he had the goods. But New York scared him." So Darryl played with local bands and eventually became a high school band director in Jim Thorpe.

Not long after, the promoter who put on Beatlefest in New York asked Denny to participate and flew him in to do the event. He figured he'd plan a few dates with his jazz trio to coincide with his trip and booked one at the Iridium and one at the Cutting Room in New York and then one at the Jim Thorpe Opera House in Pennsylvania.

Denny, the oldest child, with his parents, circa 1946. (Courtesy Seiwell Family Archive)

"It seated about 300 people in this beautiful old opera house in this quaint old antique town. They advertised us really well and my whole senior class showed up," Seiwell recalls. "We broke all the records there. And afterwards we had a table in the foyer, and I signed pictures and CDs. Darryl's two girls, Heidi and Haylee were helping me."

In or around 2015, while Darryl was living in Lake Hauto near Nesquehoning in the Poconos and Denny was playing with the Kenny Wayne Shepherd Band in Asbury Park, his little brother gathered his buddies and family to drive down from the Poconos to see Denny perform.

"They all stood in the front. The place was jam packed and I'll never forget them all standing there watching me play."

The last time Denny got to visit with Darryl was particularly memorable. Every year in Carbon County, the school district would choose their best players and put together an all-star band to perform a concert. Each band director from every school would rehearse and conduct a piece with this special band. On the 50th anniversary of this particular event, they researched the musicians and discovered that Denny had been part of the inaugural concert. They asked him to fly in to play with the band.

"What was nice is that each band director would rehearse with the band and prepare the kids for the concert. They had the music for about 120 kids. They asked me to play 'Concerto for Drum Set and Concert Band,' which was a little complicated, but the kids rehearsed quite a bit, so they had it pretty well under control. But what I didn't know was one of the band directors was a big Wings fan and he wrote out an arrangement for them to do 'Live and Let Die,' and he asked me if I would do that. I said 'What? These kids learned that?' He said they had, and I did it and Darryl conducted it."

Denny says, as a musician and a teacher, Darryl developed a lot of talented players and touched a lot of young lives.

Denny, on the other hand, was meant to be a professional player. He showed a lot of interest in music and by age 7, his father got him enrolled with the Boys Band Association in his town, where for 50 cents a week you got a group lesson and played with a concert band one night a week.

"I learned how to read music and play some marches, and within no time at all, I graduated into the senior band with the older kids who were maybe 12 or 13 years old. They rehearsed one night a week. So, for 50 cents a week I got a group lesson and two nights a week with a concert band playing marches and light overtures and things like that. We even wore uniforms and played parades and concerts in the area, so I learned how to do that."

Seiwell siblings; L-R: Paula, Darryl, and Denny in front of Magina Mancz Mansion, circa 1953. (Courtesy Seiwell family archive)

In the Boys Band Association, his teacher was Professor Charles Fronheiser, who he says was very unlike any other man in town; extremely educated and dignified with his pencil-thin mustache. By the time Denny was 13, the good professor had taken Denny through every drum book to which he had access.

"I'd stop at the band hall on my way home from school and he'd

Lehighton Boys Band spring concert covered in the local newspaper, 1956. (Courtesy Seiwell family archive)

be teaching, but he'd allow me to take other instruments home—a saxophone or a trumpet—and he'd show me how they worked and I could go home and figure it out, so I learned to play as many instruments as I could," Seiwell says, adding that he already had knowledge of piano.

Professor Fronheiser was very encouraging, recognizing Denny's talent. There was little doubt that he was far and away the best drummer in the room.

"By 13, I was playing well enough that I was getting calls to play little gigs like Elks Clubs, VFW Saturday night dances, Moose Lodges, the Orioles Club—which was a union gig, so at 13 years old they got me a special dispensation to join the union, which cost next to nothing in those days."

A guitar player by the name of Bill Rehrig, who went on to play in Nashville with Eddie Rabbitt and Dolly Parton, among others, hooked Denny up for gigs with Shorty Long, a cult hero in the country music world, early on.

Denny heard R&B music for the first time when he was 13, 14, or 15 at the Carbon County Fair, which came to the large fairgrounds down by the airport every August. Lacking the money to get in, he would go around the back of the tent and sneak underneath.

"These big trucks would come, and the sides of the trucks would open and they'd put a tent around the other side of it to have a show. Hundreds of people would be walking around on the runway. There was a Black band show too, and they would bring the band out to show you a little sample of what the show was going to be like. Some of these bands were amazing, very much like Little Anthony and the Imperials and Lloyd Price Band. These guys were working very hard. They worked all day and half the night until they shut the show down, but they'd schlep their equipment outside to play their little teaser and then back in and do their show, then take a little break and do it all over again. I was really made aware of some very serious music then. And some really funky old drum sounds. It wasn't anything like the big band music I was listening to of my dad's or anything. This was opening the door to a whole world I didn't know existed."

In high school, he played in the orchestra with timpani, bells and such, which he hadn't had with the Boys Band. "And I got to wear those silly uniforms and play the football games. One year I played football instead of playing in the band and I got beat up so bad that I said, 'Screw this, I'm going back to the band.' I was a fun-loving kid and got in trouble half the time because I was looking for things to have fun with, and the girls liked me."

He didn't get into any serious trouble, but he'd engage in silly things like tying together the front door of a history teacher's house the night before Halloween. There were three policemen on the force under Chief Joe Walsh and one of them was Denny's Uncle Tuggles Ronemus, who had to call Denny's parents more than one time to say he'd better straighten up or they might have to take him in the next time.

Mostly, Denny says he was just acting up and playing pranks, smashing pumpkins, and once in a great while he'd go up to Bill Snyder's Tavern and get a quart of beer.

"He made crab patty sandwiches, and we'd go in there and say, 'My dad wants a crab patty sandwich, Bill.' He'd go in the back to make it and we'd steal a quart of beer out of his freezer. We'd go out in the woods and guzzle the beer and then go to the Friday night dance and end up throwing up on the girls. It was all innocent childhood 16- or 17-year-old stuff."

Commander of the 6th Fleet Band aboard the U.S.S. *Springfield*, circa 1964. (Courtesy of Ken Davenport)

I'M IN THE NAVY NOW

When he got out of school, Denny would have been drafted to go to Vietnam, so he decided to enlist in the Navy. He got an audition at the Naval School of Music in Washington D.C. and was accepted into the Navy Music program which guaranteed that "I did not have to risk shooting at someone." He was required, however, to enlist for four years as a MUSN: Musician Seaman.

He had gotten engaged to his high school sweetheart right after graduation. During boot camp he found out she was cheating on him, and they broke it off. Denny got the ring back from her and sold it to a pawn shop in Chicago, getting $35 and a used watch for it.

"I wasn't a lady's man growing up, but the girls loved me because I was fun," Denny says. "I'd win dance contests because I had crazy legs, and I'd do anything for a laugh."

After Navy boot camp Seiwell was sent to the music school at Anacostia in Washington, D.C. for six months. There they put the cream-of-the-crop musicians together in a band and sent them down to Norfolk, Virginia, where they got onto a ship and sailed South America. For six months they went to such places as Trinidad and Brazil, where Denny absorbed such styles as samba and bossa nova. "This was 1963, before bossa nova was brought to America," Seiwell recalls. "This music really knocked me out. In all my time out from playing concerts in these cities, I was listening to their music and finding places where I could listen to their music. It really intrigued me. I loved it very much," says Denny.

He recalls getting off the ship in Brazil and having a little time to explore, walking down an alleyway. "I heard this great music, and I poked my head in the door. There were a few old guys sitting in there; one playing the piano, another playing a guitar, another playing a hi-hat and another playing a tambourine. It was about noon, and we walked in and the music was just great. We said, 'Hey, we too, we Bando Norte Americano.' We jumped up and start playing the instruments."

The Navy men didn't realize it was a bordello. The girls were just waking up, and upon hearing the music, they began making their way down the stairs in their robes. According to Denny, that's all it took; the music was the magnet, and the band returned each day they were there.

Denny had more musical experiences in Argentina and down to the tip of South America and Chile, as well as Ecuador. When they were playing in Chile, they had a Navy plane—a plane Denny describes as one that carries 20 or 30 people with a tail that is on the ground with its nose up in the air. "It used to fly us into places like up in the Andes Mountains," Seiwell recalls. "One of the places we landed in was Temuco, Chile, which was by the Anaconda Copper Mine. We gave a concert up there. The elevation was 11,000-plus feet. There was a little motel where we stayed, and the room key had a big rubber handle which you had to hold before you could put the key into the lock, or it would shock you and lift you right off the ground. So we were playing the concert and the trumpet player stood up to play his solo and he passed right out from the altitude. There were all kinds of experiences like that in the different countries.

"Later on, at this place in the Andes, we landed this plane in a field. I don't recall the name of the town, but there was a big hotel—the Grand Hotel—and it was old and beautiful. We stayed there, and in order for us to play concerts in the area, we had to play a concert in the hotel on the last night. We were there two or three nights, and the first night when we were done working (we were 19 years old), we asked where we could go for women and booze. They sent us to a house of ill repute, and we walked in and they were dressed to the nines! The girls immediately said, 'The bando Norte Americano!' We went up there every night. The last night was when we had to play at the hotel, and we knew we were flying out the next morning. We said, 'Ah, let's do the gig and get some sleep; we're not going to go out to the cathouse tonight.' We went to sleep and got up in the morning and we were bussed out to the airfield in the morning, which was just a field, and all of a sudden, everybody said, 'Holy shit, Davidson is not here.' One of the guys decided he wasn't going to bed when all those girls were waiting for him to go out and party. He went out to the cathouse again and apparently, they were all on top of him. We were sitting on the plane about to take off and here comes a pick-up truck flying down the road in the dust with about five or six girls, skirts flying up in the wind with Davidson sitting in the back of the truck. It was a scene from a movie; it was so good. He made it by the skin of his teeth."

Immediately after, they were in Cartagena, Colombia on November 22, 1963, when President Kennedy was shot. They were aboard the USS *Norfolk* DL-1, which was there for anti-submarine warfare with the South American navies.

"We were on operations out at sea, and when we were on operations, they put the band up on one of the flat parts of the ship and we would play marches and things for entertainment. We were highlining with the Colombian Navy tour, which was a smaller ship than ours and they would shoot a rope across. They would stabilize the rope and have a little cage where a person could sit in the cage and pass it back and forth between the ships or pass ammunition or supplies. That day we were highlining with the Colombian Navy and all of a sudden the Colombian Navy ship was getting closer to us, kind of veering in. (When you are going 30 miles an hour with a couple thousand tons of metal, if we were to collide, people would die.) It got a little too close and they sounded the collision alarm and cut the cables. As soon as that happened, everything stopped and the admiral got on the bullhorn and said they had just received communication from Washington D.C. that President Kennedy was shot and killed, so I'll never forget where I was then. Everyone was standing around crying. We pulled into port in Cartagena, and they put a moratorium on music."

Denny later played on ships all over Europe: Yugoslavia, Spain, Italy, North Africa, Casablanca, Tangiers. "We were the goodwill band. When the ship pulled in, we played concerts, the local and national tv stations, radio stations, what have you. Most of the time we were playing big band music with an augmented big band with a couple extra French horns, maybe five trumpets, five bones (instead of four). We didn't have a percussionist. It was fun because we were playing modern and contemporary music and military marches. That lasted a little too long, but it was a great training ground because it was a 24-piece big band."

He returned to D.C for several months and was then ordered to Great Lakes Naval Training Center in Chicago for a year, where he toured the Midwest with a 60-piece wind ensemble. They lived on the base in nice barracks, and they could hang out in the band room. At night the musicians were free, and Seiwell had a car, so he would drive a few miles away to North Chicago.

"There was a beautiful piano player in our band named Lanny Hartley. He was a Black musician; killer piano player, and he started playing in these little clubs like Jack's Subway Lounge which was a Blue Monday night where you would go to sit in with all these Black musicians and the trumpet player and I—this White trumpet player, Bill Shields—would migrate into Jack's Subway Lounge every Monday night. Then Lanny and some guys opened up a jazz club in North Chicago even while they were in the Navy. The club was just before Waukegan, underneath J.D's Liquor Store in a parking lot. It was quite a big space. They had Count Basie's big band there opening night, and Nancy Wilson, and some really heavy traveling jazz acts came in. But what they forgot to do was get a license to sell liquor," he says with a laugh.

Seiwell ended up getting the gig as the house drummer. He and Bill Shields were the only White faces in the establishment. It was there that Denny gained a huge musical insight. The first night of a two-night stint that alto sax player Lou Donaldson had at the club, Donaldson got up on stage. He turned around and Seiwell noted he didn't look too pleased to see him on the drums. Nonetheless, he gave him everything he had. And therein lay the problem.

"He turned around to me and gave me a dirty look," Denny recalls. "The next thing out of his mouth, on the microphone, he goes, 'Hey Leroy, come up here and get this White motherfucker off the drums!' Leroy is out there, he comes up, and I hand him the sticks and sheepishly walk over to the side of the stage to see what this guy is going to do. He sits down, they kick off the tune, and he just plays time: a cymbal beat and a cross stick on the snare drum. That was it; nothing fancy. He just shoved the time up your butt and made it feel good. And I went, 'Oh, that's what he likes, huh?' I was a lot fancier than I had to be."

The next night Donaldson showed up for work and Denny was behind the drums and took a sideways look at him. Denny said, 'Stomp it off, motherfucker.' He stomped it off and I got a big smile out of him because I gave him what he wanted. It was such a valuable lesson for me."

Denny also taught once a week at a music store owned by Frank Baumgardner in Waukegan, and he remembers eating quite a bit at the McDonald's which had just opened its doors.

Julio Coronado, a drummer and vibes player, told Seiwell he was studying drums in Chicago with Roy Knapp taught Buddy Rich, Louie Bellson and a host of greats.

"The story goes, because *Don McNeill's Breakfast Club* radio show was one of the first in America, you could say that Roy Knapp was the first recorded drummer," Seiwell says.

Seiwell can't recall how many lessons he took from Knapp, but he relished every one of them. Knapp was getting on in years and had taken a couple of falls, including one where he had broken his arm in 17 places. Yet, if Denny couldn't manage a rudiment they were working on, Knapp would insist on hopping on the drums. He'd take the sticks and execute it perfectly, even with the cast on his arm.

"He'd play it so beautifully, I'd think, 'Why do I even bother?'"

Years later, Denny was in Chicago co-producing an album for a young artist named Bill Quateman for Clive Davis. Denny and Monique weren't supposed to be there more than a couple of months, but due to unforeseen circumstances, they were there for an entire year.

"They got me a beautiful apartment on Walton Street, and one block over was Oak Street where Roy lived. Now he was in his 80s. I'd walk over and see him. One day I went over, and he was giving a kid a lesson and he was using the *Ram* album. I said, 'Roy, what?' And he said, 'You were one of my better students and I like to use the example of some of the stuff you played on the *Ram* album.' One of the nights we were there we took him down to the Happy Medium jazz club and Al Cohn and Zoot Simms were there playing. I had worked with them in New York. I said, 'Roy, can we take you down there?' He had his beret on and we took him downstairs in the club and the waitress came by and he ordered an orange juice and squeezed her ass," Denny recalls with a laugh, adding that he was told Knapp used to drink with W.C. Fields at the Chicago Stagehands Club, that Fields was a wannabe drummer and he and Knapp would hang out together and get into all sorts of trouble.

On the break, they all ended up in the dressing room with Cohn, Simms and Knapp sharing old stories. "In the midst of it, Roy started talking and they turned into little high school boys," Denny recalls. "Roy was telling stories that were from another era, and it was so beautiful."

Seiwell reflects now on the opportunities he encountered due to being stationed in Chicago for that period of time. "When I got out of the Navy, Monique and I planned on going to Chicago because the Baumgardners were planning to give me their music store, but the plans changed when I started going to the jam sessions."

His last position in the service was on the USS *Springfield* (CLG-7) with the 6th Fleet Band stationed on the French Riviera for a year and a half, and because it was the home port, the admiral let the band off four days at a time. The four band members chipped in and got apartments. "When he got off the ship there would be these little row boats and these men would pick you up off the ship and for a franc, they would row you into shore and we'd rent a little locker in this basement in Villefranche where we'd keep our civilian clothes and change into them. We'd get on the bus and leave Villefranche and go into Nice, the big city. They had a nice big USO that welcomed the servicemen that had dances at night and the local girls would come because they wanted to learn English and hang out with the sailors. There was no booze; it was very tame. It was just what you would expect it to be, a kind of safe home away from home kind of place."

MEETING MONIQUE

In France, Denny met his wife-to-be, Monique (or "Niq," as he came to call her, affectionately). She went to study English in London at 18 years old, later becoming an au pair and attending a university. When she returned to France, she started frequenting the areas in Nice where the Brits and Americans hung out to keep her English skills alive. She met Denny in 1965.

Monique, when Denny and Monique first met, circa 1965. (Courtesy of Maurice Noyer)

"I had seen her a couple of times, and she had seen me. One night I invited her to have a coffee," Denny recalls. "We had a coffee and a slice of pizza. I knew I was interested, and I knew she was interested."

Every once in a while, Denny and four of the musicians would play at the USO. Monique came to the afterparty on New Year's Eve with another musician but ended up with Seiwell that night—and that was it.

The band would be there for a week or so, then they would leave on the ship and travel around the Mediterranean doing concerts and return a couple of weeks later for another week or so. He'd rent a room wherever he could when he'd get back to town. While in town he'd also look for jazz music and jazz musicians. He discovered and played with Barney Wilen at the Loeuf (Egg)

The Navy band combo that performed for dignitary functions, 1965. (Courtesy of Ken Davenport)

Club. Wilen was born in New York, but his parents had moved to Monaco. "Over time, he was considered the Coltrane of Europe," Seiwell states.

And so it went. On that New Year's Eve, Denny knew that Monique was the one. Within a couple of months, he and Monique were engaged, and he purchased a second—and final—engagement ring. The ship was going to Barcelona, so Seiwell managed to take a little leave; Monique met him there and they had a pre-wedding honeymoon in Barcelona. At night they would go to the local jazz club, the Jazz Jamboree, where there were some great musicians like Lou Bennett, with Billy Higgins on drums. Seiwell says he actually had the audacity to ask to sit in; they'd let him and complement him afterwards. He sat in with many other legends, including a band with Booker Ervin on tenor sax and Pony Poindexter on alto. At that club Denny also had the opportunity to play with jazz pianist Tete Montoliu.

BACK HOME

In August, nine months after he met Monique, Seiwell's military duty was complete, and he returned home to Pennsylvania. He got a job while waiting for Monique's visitor's card to come through. The only work Denny could find was at a die casting factory where he would melt metal in big furnaces.

"There were big liquid metal furnaces where you would feed a bar of copper, aluminum or whatever bar of metal and you'd get a big ladle and get a big scoop of this molten metal and pour it into this machine and it would make parts for things like the bottoms of an office chair and all kinds of parts. The machine would come together on a mold and squirt the hot metal into it. My job was to melt the metal and keep the machines supplied with whatever metal they were using. You had to skim the surface of the metal for the impurities and throw that skinning over on a metal tray to let it cool down. I didn't really like what I was doing; it didn't suit me at all, and I was a little over rambunctious with the skinning the metal. When I threw it over to the metal tray, a lot of it went past the tray into the oil vent, so I almost blew the place up and burned the place down. I thought, 'I'd better get the hell out of here.'"

He stayed at the job for a couple of months, though; long enough for Monique's parents to follow Monique to town and see him holding down a respectable job that gave them the confidence to believe he would take care of their little girl.

While her parents were there, Denny and Monique decided they would get married. First they went to the Catholic church in town, but the priest put Monique through the wringer, questioning whether she really had never been married and divorced. They walked out and instead got married at Denny's church on November 26, 1966, and Monique's parents were just fine with that.

When they first got married the loose plan was to go to Chicago, where there was the possibility of the taking over the Baumgardner music store Denny had worked at while in the Navy. But when all was said and done, Seiwell was a musician; Chicago wasn't New York. He doesn't recall how he heard about a place in Whitehouse, New Jersey, called the Talley-Ho Tavern, with its Sunday afternoon jazz jams, but that seemed like a better idea.

"We drove down and it was incredible," Seiwell recalls. "All these really famous East Coast musicians would drive up from New York City and New Jersey. We went one Sunday afternoon and there was this incredible piano

Monique and Denny, 1969. (All rights reserved.)

player named John Coates, Jr., who influenced Keith Jarrett. The drummer was Tony DeNicola. There were three horn players from New York, and I had something in common with Bill Watrous, the trombone player because we were both in the Navy Band, but at different times. The saxophone player was Arnie Lawrence, and the trumpet player was Marvin Stamm (who later played the trumpet solo on 'Uncle Albert')."

Denny doesn't recall if he sat in the first Sunday he showed up or the second, but when he did, he received such encouragement from the other players that it wiped the notion of Chicago completely off the table and replaced it with New York.

At this time Denny and Monique were renting an apartment in the town of Weissport, Pennsylvania, right across the river from his hometown of Lehighton. Ben Franklin had actually once resided in the hotel-like building where they lived. "In the back of this residence was Franklin's well where he had actually drawn his water," recalls Denny.

They weren't there long before Seiwell realized he had to get out of there. They moved 26 miles away to Allentown, where they got a little apartment and a car. Denny had a buddy who got him a job at the Hammond Organ store at which he worked, which was at least related to music. They hired him as a salesman on commission; if he sold a piano or an organ, he'd have to deliver it, too.

"On the main drag, there was a restaurant bar called the Copper Kettle," Seiwell remembers. "I had balls of steel," Denny says. "I went into this place and said, 'I have a jazz trio, I'd like to come in here and play. And I didn't have a jazz trio."

To this day, he doesn't know how he did it, but he convinced two great Black musicians—Colemore Dunkin on piano and Floyd Bracey on bass—to make the 90-minute drive from Philadelphia to Allentown to play. They worked at the Copper Kettle Saturday nights for a couple of months. Although he was enjoying it, one night a week wasn't cutting it, so he paid his Uncle Bunny Snyder who worked at the musician's union in New York City a visit.

THE CATSKILLS, ETC.

"I asked (Bunny) if I could get a gig in New York City and he said to go to the 'floor' of Roseland Ballroom. Located on 52nd Street, Roseland had a big-band ballroom where people would dance, but on Wednesday afternoons, all the musicians would gather there to pick up jobs for the weekend. Sometimes the jobs were out of town, like the first job I got which was in the Catskills for five nights a week at the Browns Hotel."

He says jobs in the Catskills Mountains usually consisted of a band that would play a show for a singer, dance team and comedian. The musicians lived in the hotel in employee quarters (so Monique stayed with Denny's parents during this time) and ate in the employee dining room. It was the first time Seiwell ate gefilte fish.

"Sometimes there wasn't time for a rehearsal; you had to do (only) a talk-through, so you had to be a good reader. Hallelujah, I knew how to read music! Some of the singers in the dance teams were really hard, because the drummers had to catch all these hits as well as reading the music. Guys had written all over these charts, making their own little notes. A lot of it was very,

very challenging."

Seiwell did well in the mountains. Not only was he a good reader, but he knew how to play a show, and he became very popular. At one point singer Gloria DeHaven asked him to go on the road with her, but it wasn't as lucrative as the steady work in the Catskills.

He heard about a resort in the Poconos called the Tamiment, owned by the International Ladies Garment Workers' Union. They had an orchestra whose leader was Bob Boucher. "Now when you're in these bands that have these great players that come up there that make a great living, that stay on the property and play these shows, it's not just some chump gig. They're real studio musicians, quality players," says Denny.

The resort gave him a little cabin, so Monique was able to stay with Denny. She got a job there as well.

"I'll never forget this one night, a Broadway show came up and there might have been about 16 guys in the band. The bandstand was elevated and next to my drums was a door that went backstage. My music stand was on the left; I was playing the show and, on my right, was this door. This show came with all these beautiful girls and dancers from New York City. They would go backstage through that open door on my right, and they would strip down and get dressed in the next costume. I couldn't keep from turning to the right to watch this, even though my music was on the left, and I screwed up so royally. Afterward Bob, the leader, said to me, 'What happened to you? You usually play a perfect show!'"

They were there for about six months when Denny heard about Mt. Airy Lodge, whose drummer, Jerry Segal, who played with Charlie Parker, became unavailable. Seiwell went to work there, but they didn't have a place on the premises for him and Monique to live. The job paid well, so Denny purchased a furnished two-bedroom house trailer and parked it on Route 611, behind a gas station along with six other house trailers. He drove his Volvo to the gig each night. "They'd get big acts there like Rodney Dangerfield and Jayne Morgan," recalls Denny. "They had an opening act for us and we'd come on with the big acts." Jayne Morgan traveled with her own drummer, Danny Pucillo, with whom Denny became friends. Later, when Pucillo left Morgan, her conductor called Seiwell to do some road dates with her.

HELLO MANHATTAN AND THE HALF NOTE

One of the musicians at Mt. Airy, Dave Frishberg, told Denny that Elvin Jones was playing with the John Coltrane Quartet (minus John Coltrane) at a place called Pookie's Pub in New York City. Denny took Monique down there on a night off. The club was empty, but the band was unbelievable.

"Elvin comes off the stage and I yell out, 'Hey Elvin, I'm one of your biggest fans, man. Thanks so much for the music.' And the place is empty. 'I'm a drummer. I'd love to sit in with the band.' What was I thinking? He says, 'Sure, kid.' So, he goes back up and near the end of the set he does a long drum solo, and it is furious. The damn wallpaper is peeling off, the Richter scale is going off! Everything! And then he says, 'Kid,' and hands me the sticks. I have to say, I had balls of brass in those days. I just went up there and thought, 'I'm going to get my experience and play with the Coltrane rhythm section.' Everybody gave me that look of, 'You're alright, kid!' Afterwards Elvin and I are outside on a break and we're smoking a joint, and it's a shitty neighborhood and he's going off: 'You White motherfucker, you can play the drums!' He's doing all his Elvin schtick and I'm in heaven, absolute heaven, and then I see a rough looking dude walking down the street, getting closer and closer. This guy looks dangerous. His feet are hanging out of his shoes, his shirt is out, he's all disheveled. I'm thinking we're going to get held up, we're going to get robbed. Elvin sees him and motions him over and I realize he knows him. He says, 'Denny, I want you to meet Art Blakey.' Holy shit! (This was one of his periods where Blakey was a little nuts.) Blakey walks over and Elvin says, 'Art, I want you to meet this little White motherfucker. He plays the drums; he just played with my band!' I was in a dream.

"I owe so much of my career to three guys: Joe Beck, Dave Frishberg and Russ Savakus," Denny continues. "Russ subbed on bass one night at Mt. Airy, but was also a recording contractor in New York City, said, 'You're really a good drummer. You should come into the city, and I'll get you work in the studios.'"

One day Savakus invited Seiwell to watch Burt Bachrach's session with Dionne Warwick. "Do You Know the Way to San Jose" was being recorded at (what was then) A&R Studios on 48th Street. There was a 40-piece orchestra with Gary Chester on drums. Savakus played the string bass with Bachrach conducting.

"Gary was playing with a stick and a brush," Seiwell remembers. "Real soft, but intense. The music was so intense. I hadn't imagined how you could play so soft, yet so intense, because the microphones do all the work. It's not like a live show. I had my eyes opened to what the New York session scene was like that day. A short time after that the bandleader at Mt. Airy, Bob Newman, said some girl named Kendall Standish who was singing with us wanted to cut a demo. And we went into the city to do that; we didn't go to a local studio. We went into New York to Bell Sound on 54th Street with a couple of guys, and we cut a couple of tracks for her. That was my indoctrination to the studio."

It was Dave Frishberg who also told Denny that Mousey Alexander, the house drummer at the Half Note in New York, was about to leave. Denny went down to the Half Note and met with Zoot Sims.

Denny to Zoot: "Dave Frishberg sent me down. He said you might let me sit in."

Zoot to Denny: "Oh Sure. Any friend of Dave's is a friend of mine. What do you play?"

Denny to Zoot: "I'm a drummer."

Zoot to Denny: "Oh, I hate drummers."

That was his introduction to Zoot Sims.

And what a character! Mike and Sonny Canterino, who owned the Half Note and were the bartenders, would walk up and down in the well behind the bar to serve the customers. The stage was behind the bar.

"Zoot would drain his glass dry and just hold it up to the side and drop it," Seiwell says. "They'd see him drinking and one of them would walk by and catch it just as he was dropping it, fill it up with scotch and put it back on his drink table."

After sitting in with the band that very first night, Seiwell was offered the gig. It didn't pay much: $100 a week, 9:30 p.m. to 3:30 a.m.

"And then we would get into Zoot's old red Volvo and rush up to Jim & Andy's to make it to last call," Denny recalls. "One night we were going to Jim & Andy's and Zoot got in the back seat; he said he was tired, he was going to relax. Jack Lewis, who was a music producer that had a glass eye, was in the car and Al Cohn, who also had a glass eye, was in the car and they were both in the front seat. Zoot said, 'I'll tell you what guys, I'm gonna take a little nap. Both you guys keep an eye on the road.' Zoot was hilarious, but was nothing compared to Al. Al was probably one of the funniest cats ever. If Al and Dave Frishberg were together, you just hurt at the end of the night."

The Half Note was a great place to get noticed and Seiwell began to be the hot new guy in town. Denny says guys would come in to see who had taken Mousey Alexander's spot and Seiwell got the nod of approval. Pretty soon the news spread, and the session calls began coming in.

The year was 1968 and pop music was starting to infiltrate media like TV commercials and pop culture. It was a time when a lot of the jazz players didn't play the straight eighth-note pop music very well, but Seiwell attributes the fact that he had been so into the Brazilian straight-eighth feel to helping him get his leg up at that time. He began getting a lot of calls for the jingles and then it turned into records.

In 1969 Russ Savakus invited him to join a group of ringers to play the Peace Moratorium on the National Mall in Washington D.C.

"He sent me an airline ticket and told me when I got off the plane to look for a limo driver with a sign that said, 'Denny Seiwell and Leonard Bernstein.' He said, 'I'm sending a limo for you and Lenny.' So, I get off the plane, get my bag and I go out to the street and look for the limo driver and I go, 'What the fuck, Lenny got there before me and took the car by himself!' I got to the gig and they had a stage set up. I remember the cast of *Hair* was there and they had a tent set up. Behind the tent they had an old hippie bus parked as their dressing room. It was cold, but they were still damn near naked. We were all smoking pot, and there were cops all around. And Timothy Leary was there. Everyone was high on acid, but I was afraid of that shit! I had to play, and there was no rehearsal for this. At the end everybody got up and we did a version of 'Give Peace a Chance,' and there were half a million people swaying to my backbeat. I still get teary-eyed when I think of it."

When NBC called composer/arranger/piano player Tommy Goodman to do the Junior Miss pageant in Mobile, Alabama, he asked Denny to do the show with him. Four or five musicians from New York formed the nucleus of the band, and they used locals for the rest.

"We rehearsed for days: play-ons and play-offs, bringing the girls on and then playing off to commercials. We'd have long hard rehearsals all day long, and then after the rehearsal every night the bass player, my buddy Russell George and I would go to the Black side of town. There was a blues bar where they would play music, and we would sit in with the local cats. We were the only White guys in the place, and we'd bring some good New York pot. But what happened was there was no Black entry in the pageant and the Black Panthers took note of this. The situation was getting notice nationwide and there was a bit of a race riot on its way. Before you know it, they sent the Army down to Mobile. So, when that shit started happening, Russell and I got nervous about going back over to that place even though we loved hanging out with those cats, playing music and getting high. But we went anyway. And the Black Panthers came in that night to the club, and they saw these two White boys in the midst of everything and they said, 'Who the fuck are these guys?' All of those local musicians made a circle around us, ushered us out of the club and put us in their vehicles, took us back to our motel and stayed in the parking lot so they wouldn't mess with us."

Around the same time, in 1968, Seiwell got called to play *Jacques Brel is Alive and Well and Living in Paris*, which was off-Broadway at the Village Gate, which Seiwell says was a real treat.

In 1969 another connection from Mt. Airy Lodge, piano player Bob Dorough (who had briefly worked with Miles Davis) contacted him to work on some demos for a TV project for which he was writing clever educational music, called "Schoolhouse Rock!" The demos were so good that when the Saturday morning show began to air in 1973, they used those original recordings.

The show became an instant huge hit, with such titles as "My Hero, Zero," "Conjunction Junction," and "I'm Just a Bill." "Some people say that's my biggest accomplishment; they're more impressed with that than McCartney," says Denny with a laugh.

Years later, Denny did a little tour with Bob Dorough and the original band, thanks to an agent who had been a fan of "Schoolhouse Rock!" One of their stops was L.A.'s Troubadour in October 1996, and it was immediately sold out.

"We were watching as these kids came in with pierced ears and noses and tattoos. We started playing that 'Schoolhouse Rock!' stuff and they all turned into happy little nine-year-olds," Denny remarks with a laugh. "It was truly amazing."

In 1971, Denny got a call from a guitar player by the name of Bob Mann, whose father was a composer around town named Saul Mann. The call was to do a $1.49 Woolworth version of the *Shaft* album by the band Saul Mann and the Soul Brothers. In that band was a rookie named Will Lee on his first recording session, along with Mike Mainieri and Sam Brown. It was sensational.

"There was another time that (guitarist) Joe Beck said, 'Let's go down to the Village tonight. We're going to go down and rehearse and maybe put a band together with this guy.' I asked, 'Who's coming?' And he said, 'There's this bass player I really like playing with, Tony Levin. We're going into the Village to some loft.' I asked, 'Who are we going to play with there?' And he said, 'There's this guy named (keyboardist) Don Preston. He plays with the Mothers of Invention.'"

THAT MOTHERS GUY

Beck, Tony Levin, and Seiwell went to Don Preston's huge loft. Denny described it as having synths everywhere, along with a hippie coffee table adorned with dolls' heads on the spindle (Preston had taken them from a box of dolls that had fallen off a truck in his neighborhood). In the center hole of the table, at the top, was a green, iridescent dildo.

"He looked like a wild man, a nutty professor, with all the hair. It was the height of the Mothers," Denny comments. "We started rehearsing and we rehearsed several times. We weren't writing music as much as we were experiencing music. There were probably some outside substances present. We would start playing and then either Joe or Don would hold up their hand: a fist meant one thing, like play free, where we would go from whatever we were playing on a signal and play free, and then they would put up fingers to say to play in an odd time. It was all totally experimental, and it was fuckin' brillant!"

They called the band Ahaa, and after several rehearsals it was time to perform. They had the opportunity to play the Theatre of Living Art in Philadelphia on St. Patrick's Day.

"It was a wild theater, filled with mylar and things like that. When we got there, we had a little rehearsal time and came back the next day to play. When we got to Philly, we found out that Don had brought another person into the experience, Meredith Monk, who was an interpretive dancer, well known in the artistic community. She would paint her body red, and she wore red leather Lederhosen shorts and an engineer's cap that was red as well. While we played, she would dance around the stage and then—here's the crazy part—there was another guy, a really short guy, who stood at the front of the stage under a beach towel and as the show went on, he would slowly slide across the stage, from one side to the other. That person was Danny DeVito."

The band stayed overnight in a couple's beautiful Philadelphia 17th century home with brick and spiral staircases. Denny recalls going upstairs to use the bathroom, which was huge with a fireplace and tub, that he describes as "old and hippie at the same time." He decided to take a bath, and the woman of the couple that owned the house came into the bathroom, stripped down and got into the bathtub with Denny and proceeded to wash him.

"I didn't know what to do. I know I didn't have sex with her," says Denny, who had just recently gotten married. "She went and told her husband and everyone was laughing."

When they went to the St. Paddy's Day Parade, they were actually asked to leave.

"The whole thing was quite surreal. I remember I had an old Volvo, and I had driven down in my old Volvo and driving home my head was spinning."

JOE BECK AND THE WEST COAST

Jazz/pop guitarist Joe Beck took Seiwell under his wing. In fact, if it hadn't been for him, Seiwell may never have gotten into the Beatles. Denny was definitely late to the party, having been somewhat of a jazz elitist, but one night in late 1968 Beck invited Denny to Jackie and Roy Kral's home. They were a husband/wife jazz vocal team, and the night the four hung out, the Krals put on the Beatles recently released ninth album, *The White Album*. It was the first time Seiwell actually took notice of the band. "I said, 'Oh, is this that Beatle band?' I got deep into it," he recalls.

Beck began calling him for some great gigs, like Gabor Szabo, and they even put a band together and traveled to California for about six months in 1968 as the Joe Beck Quintet, with Roger Kellaway, Chuck Domanico and 19-year-old Tom Scott. They played clubs like Dontes and recorded records and film scores. Once in a while they would gig up in San Francisco at the Fillmore West as a rock band, the Pleasure Principle.

With Tom Scott having just come off a gig with Don Ellis, the music they were writing for Pleasure Principle was very progressive, with a lot of odd time signatures. Seiwell says Kellaway had a ballad in 11/4.

While he was out on the West Coast, Seiwell got a call from Gabor Szabo to play in San Francisco with him. Denny describes the Hungarian as a well-known junkie who was a "beautiful, beautiful guitar player who just felt too much."

He accepted the job at a place called the Matador in North Beach, which was right across the street from Jazz Workshop, where Elvin Jones was playing. He didn't ask what it paid. Szabo said, "Come on up, I got you a room and a flight," and Denny was on his way. Seiwell flew up to San

Francisco, checked into the hotel and knocked on Szabo's hotel room door.

"He comes to the door and he's all bandaged up," Denny recalls. "He had been mugged the night before. Apparently, he had been out at 3:00, 4:00 in the morning trying to score some heroin and one or two guys mugged him and shoved a gun in his eye. He thought they were going to kill him because he had money for dope. They stabbed him a bunch of times, and he said the knife blade broke on a bone in his chest. The cops just came by in the nick of time and the thieves ran off and left him. He was beat up pretty badly, with bandages around his head and chest. When he opened the door I said, 'No gig? What the fuck?' And he said, 'Oh no, hell no, we're gonna play.'"

They made it to the gig that night and Denny says the first set was absolutely beautiful. Denny thought he was amazing. "He was all hunched over, playing those beautiful lines he would play. And then on the break, we walked across the street to see Elvin as he was finishing up his set. Then he comes outside to hang out with us and Elvin picks Gabor up and throws him up in the air and says, 'Gabor you motherfucker!' And that was the end of that! Poor guy couldn't play the second set. Elvin was very physical. When he loved you, he'd give you a big bear hug and throw you straight up in the air."

When Roger Kellaway was commissioned by George Ballanchine to write a ballet, he returned to New York. Joe Beck bankrolled a trip back home in a truck with a canvas cover. Denny, Monique and Joe's friend Ginger were in the front seat while Joe sat in back with a bag of drugs and a Grecian urn that he would throw up in. They drove 28 straight hours until the car couldn't make it anymore. He recalls a memorable stop at a Southern diner for a bite to eat:

"It was the days of that Peter Fonda film *Easy Rider*. Here we were, kind of scruffy-looking long-haired hippies. We walked in and the whole place just stopped eating and turned around to look at us," Denny says. "We went, 'Oh boy, I don't think we're welcome here,' and we turned around and walked right out."

In El Paso, Texas, the truck needed service. The mechanic put the car up on a lift while the three went into the diner next door, leaving Beck in the back seat sleeping. Suddenly it occurred to them the car was up in the air and if

Beck woke up and stepped out of it, it would be a catastrophe!

They made a stop in Denton, Texas at North Texas State (now the University of North Texas) because both Seiwell and Beck had friends who were students there. Denny's friend, Jack Hanna, a former Navy buddy, was a bass player in the internationally-acclaimed One O'Clock Lab Band.

"Jack told everybody that we were New York session guys and everything, so we got to play with the One O'Clock Lab Band, which was really a thrill," Seiwell says.

They continued on to Dallas, where Beck decided he was done with the trip. He flew home from there, leaving the other three to travel by themselves. Denny says he has no idea how they even ate or paid for gas—maybe Beck had given them some money—and remembers making it to New Jersey with an empty gas tank and the girls picking up coins from the floorboards of the vehicle. The employee at the service station compassionately said, "Welcome to New Jersey."

Once back home, Denny had no lack of session work. Having befriended Mel Lewis, Seiwell was called to sub one night in the Thad Jones-Mel Lewis Jazz Orchestra at the Village Vanguard. Along with Elvin Jones, Mel Lewis was Seiwell's hero. He had met Elvin when Jones was teaching at the Pro Drum Shop, where Denny would go between sessions sometimes just to hang out with Frank Ippolito. "Papa Jo Jones would be there, and Elvin. And I'd go see Elvin in the clubs; I was a fan. And he was such a beautiful guy. His style was so unlike Mel's. Mel's style was utter taste. They called him 'the tailor' because his parts fit the song so beautifully. But Elvin was just so animalistic. So, I married those two styles to come up with my style," says Denny,

It might have been around 1969 when Lewis called Denny to sub a couple of sets at the Vanguard with the big band one Monday night, as a recording session Mel was doing was going to go late. "I walked into that place and sat down on that drum chair and all of the guys looked at me; to my left was Snooky Young and the trumpet section, and to my right was Richard Davis on bass, Roland Hanna on piano, Jerry Dodgion and Jimmy Knepper, all of these heavyweight New York musicians—and they're all looking at this kid like, 'Who the hell is this? What do we got in store for tonight?' Snooky looks over at me and says, 'Hey man, don't even look at the music, just swing.' I said, 'You got it.' I just did my Mel Lewis impersonation, but I looked over to my left at his music stand and he had the third or fourth trumpet book, so because I'm a good reader, I could see the hits coming and I started playing the music and I was starting to catch the hits with the trumpet section. I got this look of, 'Wow! Okay, kid. Nice!' What a thrill. It was such an honor to play with these guys when Mel had something else to do on a Monday night."

NEW YORK SESSION DAYS AND JAPAN

Upon his return from L.A. in 1969, Denny recorded his first jazz record called *Betwixt and Between* with Kai Winding and JJ Johnson. It was recorded at Rudy Van Gelder's studio in New Jersey. "It was phenomenal," Seiwell asserts. He notes the historical importance of this record, as he says it was one of the first to fuse jazz, rock and pop.

All day long, Seiwell was recording albums, like John Denver's first album, *Take Me to Tomorrow*, and *Gilberto with Turrentine,* by Brazilian artist Astrud Gilberto with Stanley Turrentine. He also did a tour in Japan with Gilberto

1970 tour of Japan with Astrud Gilberto. Charlie Mariano is in the foreground in the seat in front of Denny, and two rows behind him is Gilberto with her husband, Nick. (Photo by Art Koenig)

and Charlie Mariano in 1970.

Seiwell remembers a memorable flight over to Japan: "The guitar player, Paul Matzke, was seated between two nuns. He hadn't had a shower in about a week because they had turned the water off in his building. You could smell him before you could see him! We did a 30-day tour of Japan. What a great time had by all, especially the audiences.

"We would do a little jazz set with Charlie; at the time he was married to Toshiko Akiyoshi, who was a well-known jazz pianist. Charie was well-known in Japan, too; he spoke Japanese. It was the same band we played with at the Rainbow Grill in New York, but without Airto; he couldn't make it. That tour was a month long and it covered all the major cities in Japan. Toshiko was the number one star in Japan at the time, and one night she wore a crocheted dress which made it look like she was naked, but she had a body stocking underneath. When she walked out on stage that night in Tokyo, about 100 photographers came flying down to the stage and flashbulbs were going off. We played the best theaters, and it was really brilliant."

Seiwell recalls wonderful dinners and lavish hotels, but remembers the short beds on which about a foot of him hung over the bed. He said the Japanese people were lovely. He would tease them in the morning when he would arrive for breakfast at 11:00 a.m. and ask for eggs and they would say, "Oh no, no more eggs after 7:00." And he would joke, "What did you do? Lock the chickens up?"

Denny says this trip was not long after Elvin Jones and Tony Williams had been busted for drugs in Japan and they had been duly warned to be very careful when traveling over there.

"We wore sports coats to play, and every couple of nights I'd break out a different sports coat. One night I put on my Pierre Cardin sports coat, and I reached into the pocket and there was three-fourths of a fatty. This was probably about two or three weeks into the the tour. I didn't tell anyone about it, and I savored it. I would take a hit off it once in a while, put a little spit on it and dampen it and put it back in my pocket."

And speaking of clothes, there was a company that came to the hotel to design suits for the traveling acts. They would take the musicians' measurements and return two days later with the agreed upon designed suit. Denny says it was reasonable.

"I designed a suit that had tight pants with a little flared bell-bottom and a long thin jacket without sleeves and without a collar. I think the suit was $60. I had it for years. I designed some incredible shirts for $10 which, the more you washed them, the better they got."

Back in New York, Seiwell's career was picking up. His friend Bobby Gosh (piano and vocals) hired him to play a regular gig at the supper club called Jimmy Weston's. They played the tunes of the day, and it drew a great crowd. For over a year he was handling double duty: sessions during the day and the supper club at night. He'd play until 1:30 a.m. at Jimmy Weston's and be at the studio in the morning for a 9:00 a.m. jingle.

His big regret during this time was that he was working so much he couldn't attend Woodstock. His brother Darryl did, but Denny was just too busy.

THE GODFATHER OF SOUL AND MORE

What started out as a session for Hank Ballard's *You Can't Keep a Good Man Down* (released in 1969), turned into a session for two records. James Brown was producing the Ballard project when suddenly the band started fooling around on a break.

"It wasn't the song we were recording or anything, we just started grooving and James' head popped up and it was like, 'What the fuck was that?' And he came running into the studio and said, 'Hey Hank, this is too good for your record, man. This is going on my record,' and they made up the lyrics right there on the spot. That's 'The Funky Side of Town' on the *Get on the Good Foot* album," Seiwell recounts of the uncredited song on the 1972 release. "And everybody in the band was White and everybody in the control room was Black."

A typical day in the life of Denny Seiwell at that time was recording three commercials in the morning. They were one-hour bookings, which never used the entire hour and the studios were so close in proximity that he was able to schedule 10:00, 11:00 and 12:00 sessions. He would run from one to another, run across the street and throw his snare and cymbals up and his pedal down to augment the set that was there. Eventually he began bringing additional drums because he wasn't crazy about the ones the studios furnished and there was a cartage guy named Doopy who provided services.

"He would move your trap case from studio to studio with your hardware, cymbals and snare drum. I had three or four of those scattered around town chained to a pipe in the studio and we'd just leave the stuff there. We'd come in, put the key in the lock, open the lock, set the stuff up and play, throw it back into the case and run to the next studio. Anytime you needed Doopy to move your trap case, it would cost five bucks, so I said, 'What if you threw in a couple of tom toms and the trap case?' And he said, 'Make it ten bucks,' so for ten bucks I was having my drums delivered into the studios I was working in, so I had time to book them right on top of each other, which was great."

In 1970, Mel Lewis suggested to Gretsch that they endorse Seiwell, and soon after, Denny approached Frank Ippolito, who owned "the" drum store that all the drummers frequented to ask if he would talk to Remo Belli about making non-coated heads for Seiwell. He thinks he may have seen Jim Gordon playing them on a TV show. Ippolito did, and it set Denny's sound apart from other drummers. At first the engineers hated the sound, and he had to battle it out with them. They'd tell him he'd have to dampen the sound; the toms were too "live." He'd say, "Okay," and he'd tape a piece of paper towel on, and they'd tell him, "More." Denny would say, "Just try it."

"They wanted it to sound like a dead body," Denny says. "The battle continued until eventually it caught on and became all the rage. One of the guys who changed the way I looked at playing rock 'n' roll of the day was Dallas Taylor with Crosby, Stills, Nash & Young on the *Déjà Vu* album."

During one of those busy session days—that momentous day in October 1970—Seiwell stopped to use the designated phone at Jim & Andy's bar on 55th Street to check his messages with Radio Registry (the answering service most of the busy cats used). A musicians' hangout owned by Jim Koulouvaris and named after himself and his cat, Jim & Andy's was "headquarters," according to Denny. "You could go in, get something to eat, you could buy

After becoming a Wing, Denny visits that lucky place where he first picked up the fortuitous message at Jim & Andy's bar, circa 1972. (All rights reserved.)

some dope, you could cash a check, you could borrow money, you could put a band together, just about anything.

"You could even leave your equipment there between gigs locked up in the closet and if, by chance, you had your instrument stolen, Jim would say, 'What does it cost for a new one?' '$1500.' And Jim would hand out $1500 in bills. If you couldn't pay it back right away, Jim would find you a job." (Seiwell mentions a book written by Gene Lees, released in 1988 called *Meet Me at Jim & Andy's: Jazz Musicians and Their World*.)

THE INFAMOUS DAY

At the time of this memorable day, Seiwell was doing very well, getting calls for lots of jingles and recording sessions. He didn't do demos, but on this particular day, a fluke really, when he listened to his messages a session had canceled on him and there was a message saying that Barry Kornfeld, a local folkie with his finger on the pulse, wanted Seiwell to show up for an impromptu demo session in a brownstone on 43rd St., between 9th and 10th Avenue. He thought, "That's a shitty area, but what the hell?"

With no other information, Seiwell walked over to the brownstone with his cymbal bag and tom tom case. "It didn't even look like it had electricity in it. I looked up the steps; it had a lobby and there's a guy sitting at a desk. So, I walked up and asked, 'Is there a studio here?' He pointed to the basement, and I thought, 'Holy shit! I'm going to get mugged.'"

Unlike his solo debut, *McCartney*, on which Paul had played all the instruments, for his new album, to be called *RAM*, the ex-Beatle was auditioning musicians in New York to form a band for the recording. By the time Denny made it back to Jim & Andy's a few days after the audition, word had gotten out that McCartney was in town looking to make an album, but very few were admitting that they had been called in to play. No one wanted egg on their faces. Denny went back to business as usual.

Three or four days after that momentous occasion, Seiwell picked up the phone in the apartment at the Dorchester Towers at 68th and Broadway, where he and Monique had recently moved.

The voice said, "Hello Denny, this is Paul."

Denny replied, "Paul who?"

"You know, that guy from the other day?"

"Oh, that Paul!" Denny said with a laugh.

Paul said, "I want to hire you for this record. Would you want to do it?"

Seiwell continued to tease: "Give me a minute and let me see if I'm available."

He says it was the biggest surprise he ever had. He couldn't believe, with everyone in New York City, that McCartney chose him! It was, as Denny put it, "the height of Beatledom!"

The phone call from Paul McCartney asking Denny to record *RAM* was life-changing. McCartney asked Denny to commit to the project, recording at CBS from 9 a.m. to 6 p.m. for six weeks, and asked him not to take any other work. Denny found out later that Paul had booked two other drummers, but after a week of working with Seiwell, released both of them.

According to the book *The McCartney Legacy*, by Allan Kozinn and Adrian Sinclair, McCartney revealed that he had chosen Seiwell because unlike the other auditionees, Denny had gone "straight for the tom toms and within seconds the room began to throb." (Hear from the horse's mouth later in the book!)

As Denny prepared to start the *RAM* project in a few days, he got a call from Frank Ippolito, who told him the New York Museum of Famous People was closing their doors and holding an auction the next day.

Seiwell recalls, "Frank said, 'They have the Ringo drum set from Shea Stadium there. I'm going to bid on it. Would you like it? I'm not into it. I want the (vintage Ludwig) Festival snare drum, not the tom toms or the bass drum. If I get it, can I count on you to buy those from me?' I said, 'Yes! I can't afford millions.' He went to the auction, called me up and said, 'I got the set. Do you want the two tom toms and bass drum?' I said, 'Yeah! How much?' He said, '$300.' I ran down to the shop, gave him the money and took the drums home. I had my father's snare drum, and I took (the kit) to CBS Studios two days later. I set them up. They're in a drum booth in the middle of the room. Paul walks into the room, says, 'Hi man, how are you? Great to see you again. Are you ready to make some music?' I said, 'Yeah! Can't wait.'"

There was the Beatles drum set, heads and all. McCartney took a double-take before excitedly exclaiming, "Are those your drums?!"

And that was the beginning.

RAM

Although the initial reviews of *RAM* were not good, it's only because the press was decisively opinionated in a post-Beatle climate. Journalists pitted one Beatle against the other and Paul was usually the one who got the boot. In later years, all of that became much more objective and McCartney got his just due. *RAM* did indeed produce some wonderful music.

McCartney had hired David Spinozza on guitar, so on that first day, as they all went to their instruments, Paul said, "Let's see what we got here," as he began the chords to "Another Day."

Although it was not included on the original release of *RAM*, subsequent editions and compilations have added the song. It was McCartney's first actual single and it went to No. 5 on the U.S. charts.

Seiwell says he and McCartney had an immediate, telepathic musical connection, and that any of Paul's performances on piano, guitar and vocal could have been the final take.

Seiwell remarks that "Another Day" changes time signatures, going from 3 (a waltz) back into 4. "Spinozza and I looked at each other like, 'Shit, this is not your typical recording session! This music is great.'

"In the back of my mind I knew this was historical," Seiwell recounts. "Just because it was Beatle Paul. I knew from his songwriting that this music would

Paul and Denny doing percussion overdubs for the *RAM* album at CBS Studios, 1971. (© 1971 Paul McCartney / Photographer: Linda McCartney. Under exclusive licence to MPL Archive LLP)

not be over and done with in 50 years. I believe in another 50 years, they will still be playing this music, because it was a period filled with angst. Linda got him off his ass in Scotland or he would have just sat up there and drank and played his guitar, played with the kids, sheared a few sheep and waited for the Beatle thing to be over. But she said, 'You're a musician. Let's go to New York and make a record.' So, God bless Linda and God bless him for knowing she was right."

Linda McCartney, Denny says, was not involved at all on the tracking sessions for *RAM*. (She would later overdub background and co-lead vocals on "Long Haired Lady.") She made tea for the musicians, although Paul would ask her opinion consistently.

"Little Mary was my girlfriend," Denny says. "She would hop up on my lap every time I came in. Every once in a while, she would sit at the drums, and I would put the sticks in her hands. Heather was there too."

They ran through "Another Day" a couple of times, turned the machines on, recorded a few takes, and that was that. "See you guys tomorrow."

There was a section in the song that needed a sound like horses' hooves. Woodblocks and tambourines were not the instruments that were going to provide the sound Paul had in mind. Seiwell began to look around the studio.

"I found the Manhattan telephone directory, which at the time was about 3 inches thick. I put it on a stool and played it on that part, and it's on that recording," Seiwell recounts.

When Seiwell and Fernando Perdomo recorded the 2021 tribute album *Ram On,* he asked drummer friend Billy Amendola to record that part, but with 1971 Manhattan phone directories no longer available, Amendola had to put two current thinner directories together for the recording.

Seiwell says they never did more than four or five takes on anything. "It was a fantastic experience. I couldn't wait to get to work the next day. I couldn't wait to get out of work and stop by Jim & Andy's, have a drink and tell the guys what I had been up to."

Some of those guys included Gary McFarland, Don Payne, Ronnie Cuber,

Joe Beck and the bartender Rocky. "Rocky would smoke a cigar and Gary would come in and say, 'Give me a cognac, no ashes this time.'"

Everyone wanted to know what it was like working with Paul McCartney, and Denny would say, "It's phenomenal. It's like nothing I've ever done."

Elaborating further, Seiwell says: "There's a different head space that comes from playing in a band as opposed to playing a session. This was more like playing in a band because he brought his Beatles disciplines. It wasn't like a bunch of musicians with music charted in front of them. We were creating together. He didn't tell any of us what to play. Except one time."

That was on the multi-segmented "Uncle Albert/Admiral Halsey," the first of McCartney's post-Beatle no. 1 Billboard hits. It was the only track on which Paul gave Seiwell any direction. "Paul said, 'Instead of playing a regular drum beat there, can you play something there, can you play something that kind of goes around the vocal; something not so ordinary.'"

Instead of just timekeeping on the snare, he describes the pattern he ended up with: "Ride cymbal on 1, snare drum on 2, the floor tom would play three beats, and an open hi-hat on 4. And it left all this space for the vocal that would have been covered up if it were just straight time. So I left all this space for the vocals to appear. It didn't take me long to come up with it. I don't know how it came to me, but Paul smiled; he loved it immediately."

That opened the door for the freedom to play even more creative drum parts and some fun experimentation.

As soon as he heard "Heart of the Country," Seiwell thought of brushes. In the control room, he found some bits and pieces of thin sheet metal laying around. He hit a piece of sheet metal with the brush and liked the sound.

"I probably laid a towel on my snare drum and put the sheet metal down and had that as the snare drum, and there was a microphone right there. I used that and then instead of the bass drum, I used a plastic waste can and taped my pedal to it and did the country kind of beat. I taped up my hi-hats, too, so they sounded very dry and dead, and I taped up some cymbals as well. I turned the time around occasionally and then the engineer put some echo on all of it. The tapping is Paul's foot, I think—a cowboy boot on a hardwood

Paul showing another masterpiece to Hugh McCracken and Denny on a *RAM* session in 1971 before recording with the boys. (© 1970 Paul McCartney / Photographer: Linda McCartney. Under exclusive licence to MPL Archive LLP)

floor," Denny says with a laugh.

Throughout the sessions, Denny would change the tuning of the drums. "If the song was in a specific key, I would try to tune my tom toms so they would be within two notes of that scale. If it was in C, I would try to make the floor tom C and the top tom F or G, so they were notes of the scale of whatever the song was in. Then I would tape it up and turn down the bottom head so the sound would be a floppy sound, kinda like Ringo. I was stealing some ideas of what I thought they might have done in the Beatles. I would do that on each song—alter the sound of the snare drum and the tom toms."

Denny only owned four cymbals at the time: a set of hi-hats, a 16" Zildjian he took from the Navy when he left, and a 20" ride he bought from Frank Ippolito's. That set of cymbals, minus the 16" Zildjian and the Leedy snare drum his father gave him, was sold to the Hard Rock Café along with his "Live and Let Die" set.

Midway through the recording of *RAM*, Spinozza was let go. According to Seiwell, there were a couple of reasons.

"Spinozza was wild," Seiwell recalls. "He didn't care that this was Paul McCartney. We would go in to listen to a playback and he would fool around, which was unexpected. He was very loose, and you could see Paul was uncomfortable. And Paul started seeing that sometimes he would leave after lunch early, so Paul could see he had taken a session. One day, Spinozza said, 'Can you cut me loose today? I have something else I have to do.' Paul didn't like that. That's when he asked me if there was another guy I worked with who would fit in, and I suggested Hugh McCracken."

In that six-week period, Seiwell believes they recorded about 23 tracks for the album and Seiwell says it was a very enjoyable experience. They even shared some meals together. One night McCartney reserved a private dining room at Luchow's, and they all crammed into a limousine to dine at what was once an elegant celebrity favorite. Another night, Denny recalls, they finished late and all went down to Chinatown to a restaurant called The 68 on Mott Street. "We were mates making what we knew was a beautiful record. It was just so natural," Seiwell says. He says they didn't talk about the Beatles at all. It seemed to be a subject that was stuck in his throat, a tough topic for McCartney. "He would come to work every once in a while and you could tell he had had a rough night. He was more interested in the present. And you know how it is, the grass is always greener: the New York musicians were so much better, and the New York musicians thought the English musicians were so much better."

One of Denny's favorite tracks recorded in that period, "Oh Woman, Oh Why," was not on the original release, but was included in the Special and Deluxe editions of the 2012 remasters of *RAM*. "It was rock 'n' roll, it was really groovin', it was tough and mean. I thought that was the direction we were going to go in after all the epic songs like 'Uncle Albert' and even 'Too Many People,' 'The Back Seat of My Car,' 'Long Haired Lady,' those kinds of tracks. So, when we got to doing 'Oh Woman, Oh Why,' I thought, 'This is the rock 'n' roll that the Beatle fans are going to love.' That's why it's my favorite track. It's a simple song. The vocal is sensational. I love 'Monkberry Moon Delight,' too. I did love 'The Back Seat of My Car,' too. Those epic pieces that had so many movements in them were more challenging as a drummer to get it right and make that track mean something, and it was something totally unique to any of the other work I was doing. So every day doing something like 'Long Haired Lady,' 'The Back Seat of My Car,' 'Uncle Albert,' 'Little Lamb Dragonfly' (which was recorded during *RAM* but released on *Red Rose Speedway*), you almost needed a chart to guide you through the different sections of them, but we didn't have any of that. There was none of that, and we didn't use any click tracks. We rehearsed the song until everybody felt good about what we had and it all fit nicely together, and we started making takes."

Seiwell mentions "Too Many People" as one of the memorable tracks. There are no drums at the beginning of the song, and then he says he entered with what was, for him, a unique drum part.

"You take the first part of the song, which we will call the verse, and you play something that is totally unlike a regular drum part, and then when it gets to the chorus it becomes more of a normal thing. All the time you're paying respect to the song and supplying the rhythmic basis for the song itself. '3 Legs' was interesting because it was really sparse. Each track I had to come up with a part that wasn't a regular drum beat, so I had to listen and play around the melody."

For "Long Haired Lady," Denny says he had to come up with several different parts. There are sections with no drums; they come in and then go out again.

He describes "The Back Seat of My Car" as three or four different movements with not one regular part. "At the end of the song there is a drum fill that is probably my favorite drum fill of all time."

Seiwell is not on "Ram On." McCartney played drums on that song. "He had a floor tom and he was stamping his foot. When you hear 'Ram On,' he had hand claps, foot stomps and it was written as a commercial for the album, I think."

According to Seiwell, Paul was very humble. He did not carry with him any sense that he had changed the face of music.

"One day on *RAM*, we had come back from lunch. I think it was a Friday because I can remember that the engineers had begun to tear down the mics. Paul was wound up and he picked up this green and black Firebird guitar he had and started slamming away. He looked over at me, and I went over to the drums and started playing. The engineers were like suit-and-tie guys, the EMI guys. They weren't jumping fast enough, and we were looking at them like, 'Come on guys, get the mics working.' We had already played about 10 minutes when they said, 'Okay Paul, we're ready now.' So, we did take two. Take two wasn't just *slammin'*..."

That was "Rode All Night," which found its way into the world of bootlegs, officially released in 2012.

Shortly after Seiwell returned to his session work, concert promoter/producer Michael Lang brought Seiwell a new artist named Billy Joel to produce. He was halfway through Joel's first album *Cold Spring Harbor* at a Long Island studio called Ultrasonic Recording, when he got a call from McCartney to finish *RAM* in L.A. Denny asked him if it could wait until he finished the Joel project, but when McCartney said no, he had to leave it behind.

"I wasn't smart enough to sign him up to a production deal or anything. I loved him, he was so talented," Seiwell says.

FINISHING *RAM* IN L.A.

Denny is pretty sure Paul chose L.A. over New York because of the weather. It was February, and New York was no fun that time of year. One night while they were recording *RAM* at CBS Studios in New York, Seiwell recalls, it was pouring rain as they were leaving the studio at rush hour. Paul and Linda were living on the Upper East Side and it was tough getting a cab.

Denny asked him what was going on and Paul said, "I can't get home. I can't get a car to pick me up, I can't get anything because of the rain."

"I said, 'Really?' I said, 'Hang on a second.' I called Joe from Lomto Cabs, the checked cab company from Queens, I think. I said, 'Red,' (He was the dispatcher.) 'Hey Red. I've got Paul McCartney here. He can't get home. You need to send a cab to 52nd street and pick him up at CBS and take him up to 85th street.' He said, 'Tell him to go out front.' I said, 'Paul, go out front. There's a cab company coming to get you by the time you get out there.' And by the time he was out front, there was a cab waiting for him. The next day he said, 'What are you? The mayor of this place?'"

Upon his arrival in Los Angeles, they went into Armin Steiner's Sound Recorders and recorded "Dear Boy." McCartney brought Jim Guercio (Chicago) in to produce. "He wanted to get the drums in stereo; he wanted a weird kind of stereo effect, so he took half the stuff away, so if I was going to play the ride cymbal and snare drum the first time, he would take the tom toms away," explains Seiwell. "He would put the stuff back and then if I was going to play kick drum and tom toms, he would take the other shit away. I'd be air drumming the shit that wasn't there. It was so weird that Paul and I kept looking at each other. It didn't make any sense. I kept doing it and pretended to play the part because I knew the part, but it didn't work out. I remember sitting in the lobby when Paul was telling him it wasn't going to work out. I didn't want to be a fly on the wall there. Nobody knew how to produce Paul McCartney better than he knew how to produce himself," says Denny. "That was the end of Jim.

"Paul had a guitar that he tuned all on the same note, and on 'Dear Boy' he held the guitar out for me and I took very light timbale sticks and I played across the strings so the sticks touched all the strings at the same time. It's a very unique sound on that track. I don't recall whether it was his idea or mine. I think we ended up using the part that Guercio painfully extracted from me."

During their time in L.A., Denny and Monique accompanied the McCartneys to the Grammy Awards on the fly.

"He said, 'Come with us,'" Seiwell recalls. "We had nothing to wear. So, we scrambled and went out looking. I went down to Santa Monica Blvd. to some hippie store and bought a purple leather jacket. I had a light lavender colored shirt I had made in Japan in 1970 when I was over there with Astrud Gilberto, and I bought a Peter Max tie. That was my outfit for the Grammys. Everybody was wearing tuxes in those days. Paul had on a tux jacket with no shirt and a plastic bow tie. We sat in the very back of the room at a table for four with a red-and-white checkered tablecloth. There were little pop-up artists like Aretha Franklin singing 'Let it Be,' or Conway Twitty singing all around the audience. I remember being very impressed with Twitty. We met there, and the press was taking pictures of all of us. They called the award for

'Let it Be,' Paul and Linda went up and got the award, then they went out the back, and we never saw them again that night. We walked back to the hotel."

Denny and Monique were staying at a local motel, although McCartney did rent them a car while they were in town. The McCartneys rented out J. Paul Getty's house on the Pacific Coast Highway along the beach. Denny recalls visiting them there one evening.

"I remember eating something, hanging out with the kids, and going in the pool, which was behind the house," Seiwell recalls.

A week or two after finishing up *RAM,* Seiwell went back to New York and his previous life. The album was released in May. He remembers one day the doorman calling up to his apartment on West 68th Street saying he had a delivery. It was a box of *RAM* LPs. "I put it on the turntable and listened to it. I had never heard him play the bass," Denny reveals. "It had been three musicians, Paul playing the guitar, I was playing drums and Dave Spinozza or Hugh McCracken playing the other guitar part. That was it. There was never a bass player on the tracking dates. So, he was recording all his bass parts after we left at night—off of the bass drum parts that I had created. Listening to the album was the first time I heard them. I was blown away."

WON'T YOU COME TO SCOTLAND?

Denny figured once *RAM* was released, that was that, but a few months later, sometime between June and August, McCartney called and invited the Seiwells to Scotland. Paul didn't say why, but Denny and Monique figured they'd combine it with an opportunity to visit Monique's family in the south of France.

Once they arrived, just making their way to High Park, the McCartney farm, was an adventure. It was out in the middle of nowhere. When they asked the townspeople how to get there, they said, "Oh, it's kinda tricky. You take this little back road, and that little back road, and then you see a farmer's house. You'll have to honk the horn and get the farmer to tell you how to get the lane that goes up to Paul's place."

The Seiwells rented a car. "Here's me right off the plane from New York and I'm in a left hand-drive car. Thank God I didn't kill anybody that first day, and we proceeded to make our way and finally reached the farmer. He said, 'Can I help you?'" Denny recalls. "I said, 'Yeah, we're trying to get up to Paul's place. Can you tell us which road to take there?'" What followed was in a Scottish brogue so thick it was barely intelligible, but Denny says he made out the words "back lane" and he drove on up the dirt road. "You had to open gates and then close them because there were animals all over. Then you drove up further and there were more gates to open and close. And I was beating the shit out of this poor rental car, going over big rocks."

At Low Ranachan barn on Paul's other property where the band rehearsed through the years. (Photo by Trevor Jones)

The Seiwells arrived a day before the McCrackens, so McCartney spent the time showing them around the house and its surroundings. Denny describes the house as a simple two-bedroom: one for Paul and Linda, another for the two kids (Stella had not been born yet) and a kitchen. It had pine walls, concrete floors and sparse furnishings.

"They had a kitchen table and some chairs. I don't recall a couch or a TV or anything," Seiwell remarks. "It was very rustic. He showed us the barn, which was a small lean-to, which was Rude Studios. He had it finished inside so it had some sound quality about it."

McCartney showed them the pink tractor that his wife bought him on one of his birthdays.

"They had five or six old racehorses that they had rescued. One was called Honour, one was called Drake's Drum, another was Cinnamon, and I think there was a pony that the kids could ride around on, and then Martha (My Dear), of course, the sheepdog, and they had a dalmatian puppy named Lucky. He was showing us all the animals and he took us out to the pen to where the sheep were. He flipped a sheep over, took one of the shears and showed us how they shear the sheep. He showed us how the men would go from farm to farm and shear sheep all day long, get a quart of Scotch whiskey and then go in the barn and sleep on the fleece and get up the next morning. They'd feed them and they'd go on their way to the next job."

McCartney also showed them the standing stone just outside his farm, which was a large stone, 20 or 30 feet tall, surrounded by little boulders.

"He explained to me that this was how the Druids set up their first calendars. They would line the stones up with the top of the standing stone and the stars, and that's how they would figure out what day, month or week it was. There was a vibe there in Scotland, especially at dusk, you would really feel some shit. Then Paul would tell me some stories about how one tribe would attack another tribe and all this crazy stuff. It was a very wild and unique place."

The McCartneys had a man who worked for them named Duncan, who built a road from their small farmhouse about a quarter of a mile down the hill to another much bigger, but dilapidated, two- or three-story farmhouse that McCartney owned, called Low Ranachan. Duncan, he says, was tougher than rope. "After he built the road, he lined both sides with boulders. It would take three men to pick up one of those boulders, but he did it himself," Seiwell notes.

Next to that farmhouse was a big barn with two stories which is where the band rehearsed for the *Band on the Run* album (which Denny did not actually end up recording, but we will get to that later.)

"This barn actually had good acoustics. He brought a 2-track over there and recorded the band before we went down to London to record *Band on the Run* (which they did in Africa), but somewhere in the universe there is a 2-track of the band in that barn at Low Ranachan. The word is that he had that 2-track transferred over to cassette, which he took down to Lagos so he would have references, because he played all my drum parts."

The McCrackens arrived the following day and joined them at the little Argyll Arms Hotel Campbeltown, which had no heat. They had to put hot water bottles between their legs while they slept. The location, however, was beautiful, on the ocean, with little villages all around them. There was a little island close to the coast owned by Jack Bruce that you could walk to at low tide. The Campbeltown Picture House, built in 1913, was one of the earliest cinemas in Scotland. Then the following day, the four went up to McCartney's Rude studio which was filled with instruments. They played a little, drank a little and had some fun.

"That night, Paul said, 'I miss having a band and being in a band,'' recalls Denny. "Would you be interested in forming a band?' And I said, 'I'm in.' I loved working with him. Hughie said, 'Can I think about it tonight?' So, Hughie and Holly went back to the hotel where we were all staying, and Linda said, 'Can you come back tomorrow and leave the wives at home?' Holly didn't like that much—and I don't think Monique did either, but Linda was that way."

McCracken and Seiwell went back up to the McCartney farm the following day. They made some music and hung out. Paul broached the subject of the band once again: "What do you think about making this a band?" McCracken said, "I don't think I can do that."

Monique and Denny enjoy the rustic life of Scotland, circa 1972. (Photo by Hugh McCracken)

Seiwell recalls: "I was shocked. Paul was shocked. No one ever said 'no' to Paul. He didn't know what 'no' was. They left and we went back to New York. A couple of weeks later, Paul called and said, 'Come back, I've got Denny Laine, this guy from the Moody Blues and we'll make it a band.'"

The Seiwells packed up and sold everything to an up-and-coming young drummer named Rick Marotta, who had just moved to New York. "We had a beautiful little apartment full of designer furniture, TV, stereo, Wurlitzer piano. I kept hearing about this kid who sounded like me. I told all these jingle people I worked for every day to start calling this guy, because I was going to England to play with a Beatle. They said, 'Go!'"

Denny says he felt it was "my ticket to ride."

A NEW CHAPTER

McCartney knew Denny Laine from earlier days, when the Beatles were young. Laine was in the Moody Blues and their paths were crossing. Seiwell surmised that McCartney wanted someone like Lennon to bounce things off and someone who was "a bit of a loon, with a sense of humor."

Now with two Dennys in the band, for some time McCartney would call out their name and both of them would turn around, until he decided that he would call Seiwell, at 6'-2.5" "Big Denny" and the 5'-7.5" Laine "Little Denny."

Seiwell mentions the well-known fact that British folks are slow to warm up to people. "Paul warmed up because he had a different kind of background," Denny says. "But Denny Laine was a little cautious when he came in, and it took some time."

The Seiwells had been paying their own bill at the Argyll Arms Hotel. In fact, they were paying for everything; they had paid for their flight over there. So, they decided to finally put an ad in the *Campbeltown Courier*, which came out every Thursday: "Young American couple wants to rent a farmhouse" and they were contacted by the McMillan Family. They took the rental car out to the Breakachy Farm Kilkenzie, about eight miles from Campbeltown.

The woman explained there was a furnished house on their property where relatives had lived but had now passed away. From the dining room Denny says you could see the ocean, which was about a mile away, and "to the left it looked like the white cliffs of Dover. The coastline just went up as far as the eye could see on the right. It was just fabulous. And on a clear night or a clear day, you were 28 miles across from Ireland, so you could actually see Northern Ireland.

"The house had a large room with bedrooms all around it. The main room had a Rayburn coal stove in it. That was your dining room, and next to that was a small kitchen area. I think there was a small fridge. There were three small bedrooms off the main room. We asked what kind of rent she would need, and she said, 'Would 5 quid a week be asking too much?' Five quid a week was $12.50. So, I paid her for the first six months."

They found a piano for sale in the *Campbeltown Courier*, which Seiwell arranged to buy and have delivered by the people who delivered coal.

Breakachy Farm Kilkenzie, Campbeltown, 1971.

On the roadway at the farm the Seiwells were renting, circa 1971.

The multi-purpose dining room in the Scotland farmhouse, 1971.

Denny at the farm with his 1953 Land Rover and Circles, the cat. (All photos this page by Monique Seiwell)

"While I was in there, I looked at this beautiful hand-carved bureau behind the desk where this guy was and I said, 'I'll give you another 5 quid if you throw that sideboard on the truck.' He said, 'Make it 10 quid and you have a deal.' This thing was worth thousands. All that went into the dining area with the coal stove and the other little bedrooms had a tiny fireplace that burned coal. Then we said, 'We gotta get a TV,' so we had some guy in the village come out and install an antenna on the roof and we bought a cheap TV, probably a black-and-white, and he put an antenna on the roof. In those days in London and anywhere in the British Isles, you would get three channels, but to his surprise, we got five channels: BBC1, BBC2, STV (Scottish TV), and then two channels from Ireland, so I could see what was going on in the U.K. and in Ireland as well. I'm sure we were the only people up there who had something like that. You know Americans, they have to have their fuckin' TV! Now we have nice furniture, a piano, a TV and then we had to have a phone put in, so Paul could call us. I don't remember Paul's number, but our number was Kilkenzie 2, 3, 5."

The next obstacle was procuring transportation since Denny had ruined three or four rental cars traveling over boulders getting up to McCartney's place. The rental car places would no longer rent to Seiwell, so he placed an ad in the *Courier* to purchase one. He ended up with an old used 1953 canvas-backed Army-style jeep that he says "ran like a top." When they left Scotland, he bequeathed it to Duncan.

The Seiwells offered Laine a place to stay so he didn't have to incur the cost of a hotel, so Laine and his Dachshund dog (named Ahh Kid) came to stay in one of their bedrooms. Monique cooked for them and all was well, and he stayed for quite a while—until Monique began to feel a bit like a maid and it was time for Laine to go.

They rehearsed in the McCartney lean-to—Rude Studios—for a couple of weeks to learn to play some of the songs, like "Bip Bop" and "I Am Your Singer," for the *Wild Life* album. Denny says "Some People Never Know" was recorded during the *RAM* sessions and "Tomorrow" had begun at that time as well.

It was when they began to rehearse that McCartney broke the news that his wife was going to be the keyboardist in the band.

"Nobody said anything," Seiwell says. "On the last trip before Hugh McCracken came over, we talked about it and I told him about a great piano player named Paul Harris who I worked with a lot in New York," says Seiwell, adding that he recalls McCartney saying, "I can teach her what she has to know. She has great rock 'n' roll sensibility."

"Having seen this guy in action through the whole *RAM* period, I believed him 100% that he could teach her the simple parts, because what he played as a Beatle—his songwriter/piano parts—were just well thought-out and simple that anyone could play them," Denny states. "After spending time with him, I knew he could pull it off and it would be great. You really didn't have to be an accomplished musician to play the music we were playing, as long as it came from the heart, and you knew what you were doing chordal wise and everything."

The very beginnings of Wings at McCartney's Rude Studio at his farm in Scotland. (© 1971 Paul McCartney / Photographer: Linda McCartney. Under exclusive licence to MPL Archive LLP)

WILD LIFE

It turned out a little bumpier than McCartney thought it would. Linda was not initially well accepted by the press or the fans, but on August 31 the band proceeded to London to record *Wild Life.* All four band members sat around trying to name the group. Everything was a band process. Denny says McCartney wanted it to be just like the Beatles where John, Paul, George and Ringo made the big decisions together. So for days, they racked their brains to come up with monikers. Denny says they came up with some pretty lame ideas, although the only one he can remember now was the Dazzlers, he offers with a big laugh.

Paul announces the new band Wings at the Mecca ballroom in London in 1971. (Promotional photo)

"We couldn't come up with something good, for the life of us. It was terrible. They had the Silver Beatles before they had the Beatles, but then Paul said, 'We took a name that didn't mean anything and then we made that word mean something.'"

On September 13, while Linda was giving birth to Stella, there were complications and she needed an emergency Cesarean section delivery.

"When Linda had this difficult birth and Paul said Stella was delivered like on the wings of an angel, he said to us, 'Wings – that's a pretty nice word. Let's just make that the band name and we'll make the word wings mean something.' Everyone agreed."

Seiwell had to join the British union and, of course, the government didn't like an American taking a job away from one of their own, but McCartney fought that battle. He told them, "I don't want a British drummer; I want this guy!"

At the time they were in London, the pay for musicians in New York was $90 for a 3-hour session. In the U.K., it was $30, but thankfully when they went in to make an album, they racked up a lot of hours. Like most government payments, it didn't come quickly, but when it came, it definitely helped.

They stayed at a quaint British hotel a couple of blocks from EMI Studios called Swiss Cottage, with Denny again paying with his own credit card. (Later on, Denny says, he did bring it up to McCartney who told him to make a list of expenses, and he would reimburse him.) It was within walking distance of the studio.

"It was that weird period of time when they said there was no money," Seiwell says. "On one hand I wanted to be there 100%, but on the other hand I was thinking, 'Something's not right here. This guy should be a billionaire. He shouldn't have to even think about money.'"

They rented Denny a set of Ludwig marine pearl drums for the sessions, to be recorded at EMI Studio 2, which later, of course, became Abbey Road. Seiwell believes he brought in his Gretsch drums, as well and used pieces of both kits on the tracks.

"The sound of the room with that high ceiling was nothing like any studio I had ever been in," Denny comments. "It really had its own life. It was steeped in history, and it was amazing."

In the beginning of September, while Paul and Linda were having a baby, Denny and Monique took a little trip to New York and returned on October 1, Monique's birthday. They flew back on a redeye and took a cab directly to Osterley Park for the *Wild Life* album cover shoot. Then they went back to the Swiss cottage for a few days, and the band went back to work on the record. While they were recording, Monique scouted the area, and on October 6, she secured a rental on Draycott Place so the Seiwells could get out of the hotel.

"It was just one large room near Kings Road," Denny recalls. "Again, the office didn't help, and we were making no money—70 quid a week—which is $175 a week. We stayed there for a couple of months."

Although they only had parts of a couple of the songs, five of the eight songs were first takes. "That means the rhythm track was performed well enough that we could go back and fix little mistakes and then overdub on top of it," Seiwell clarifies. "Paul wanted the band to have a first look at the music without all the polishing that went into making records."

McCartney asked Denny to keep his ears on the vocals as they were being recorded, so he'd go into the booth and listen to the singers with the engineer.

"Working with Paul, his vocals were amazing, even his harmonies, just him, were unbelievable. He sang so in tune and so effortlessly. Any time I could do that, it would justify all of the heartache and all the difficulties I had to endure to be there. I knew I was making musical history."

They were working up a rocker one day that became "Mumbo," and on the track you can hear McCartney say, "Take it, Tony."

"That's Paul telling the engineer (Tony Clark) to turn on the fucking machine and record, because we were just jamming. That's how that song came about," Seiwell recalls. "We wanted to do a version of Mickey and Sylvia's 'Love is Strange,' but we wanted to do it differently, so we said, 'Let's do it reggae.' We were coined as the first white rock 'n' roll pop group to even attempt reggae. We had some fun with it and came up with all the different sections of it, and to this day I get emails from drummers around the world about that song. It was just on the fly."

On October 26, they all went back to Scotland and the Seiwells had dinner at the McCartney farm. Denny finally broached the topic of money. Right after that, he received a reimbursement of 800 pounds, representing the hotel bills and airfare expenses. That was a lot of money, considering Denny was only earning 70 quid per week.

Shortly after that, the Seiwells took a vacation to Nice to visit with Monique's family, then a short trip to Liverpool to meet Paul's father, and then they returned to London to work on *Wild Life* overdubs.

McCartney threw a big party on November 8,1971 to announce the formation of Wings at the Empire Ballroom. Paul sported a Tommy Nutter unfinished suit, while Linda wore a designer dress with moccasins. Denny says he went in fairly normal attire: sports coat and turtleneck sweater. Monique wore a stylish dress from Antiquarius. Attendees included members of the Who, Led Zeppelin, the Faces, Peter Frampton, Elton John, Ginger Baker and more.

The album was not yet finished, but McCartney wanted the world to know there was about to be a new band with which to be reckoned.

On the 24th the Seiwells were in New York when they received a call from McCartney asking Denny to take the *Wild Life* tapes to Sterling Sound to be mastered for the American release. Seiwell said, "Are you sure you want me to do this? That sounds awfully important!" But McCartney said yes, "Just go in there and make sure it sounds big and fat; you have good ears."

So, Denny picked up the tapes at Apple and brought them to legendary George Marino at Sterling Sound. He then returned the masters to Apple.

"We walk into Apple, and I run into John Lennon and Yoko. John looks at me and says, 'Ugh, you're Paul's new drummer, eh?" That was it. They were walking out, and I was walking in. It was a nasty time.

The album was released in the U.K. on December 3 and in the U.S. three days later.

The McCartneys arrived in New York City, first to finally have a face-to-face with Lennon and work out the Beatles' legal situation, and then to do some recording and rehearsing with Wings. During the New York trip, the band went into A&R Studios to overdub on "Blues," a *RAM* leftover track to be retitled "The Great Cock and Seagull Race." Seiwell recalls the whole band piling into a limo the night of December 17 and going down to Chinatown for dinner. The following day they began rehearsals at David Lucas' studios.

When they returned to London, McCartney said he felt they needed a lead guitar player to fill out the band, and the name Henry McCullough came up. McCullough had been playing with the Grease Band, Joe Cocker's previous backup band, which Denny describes as a really good, soulful country, bluesy English Irish rock band. When McCullough was suggested, McCartney told one of the roadies, Ian Horne, to call him up, and the guitarist came into the little theater at which they were rehearsing. The fit was right immediately.

"After five minutes of playing, we all looked at each other like, 'Uh-huh, that's the guy!'" Seiwell recalls. "I really loved Henry at the time. Later he became a bit of a problem because of his behavior."

Illustrating his point, Denny recalls a story: "Paul called me one Christmas Eve or New Year's Eve when Henry and (wife) Sheila went to visit them in Liverpool, while they were visiting Paul's father, and they were out in the street fighting. Monique and I were in New York and Paul called me from Liverpool and said, 'I don't know what we're going to do about Henry,' and I said, 'It's not my week to watch him.'"

"GIVE IRELAND BACK TO THE IRISH"

Questionable behavior aside, on January 1972 McCullough joined Wings. When all hell broke loose January 30 in Northern Ireland, on what would become known as "Bloody Sunday," McCullough's first project with Wings would be the controversial song "Give Ireland Back to the Irish," recorded at EMI Studios on February 1, released on February 25.

"Paul called us all up to the house and the roadies, Ian Horne and Trevor Jones, brought all our gear up there and set it up in the living room. Paul had written the song, and I thought the situation was awful, of course, but to be honest, I didn't know the history of 800 years of the British government putting their fingers on the neck of the Irish. We didn't talk that much about it. Paul wasn't really into making political statements, but he had to because he felt ashamed by what his government had done."

Denny says McCartney was not concerned about it being controversial or banned—which it was in Britain. But ABC News came to McCartney's house, where they filmed the band performing it live, before they recorded it at EMI (which later became Abbey Road).

They discussed what in the world they were going to put on the B-side of the single, and they took a tip from the old Jamaican records that would put the same song sans vocals on the B-side. So, McCartney had the idea to take the rhythm tracks and replace the vocals with Irish penny whistles for the B-side version.

Soon after, McCartney said, "Let's just go someplace, play universities and keep it under wraps. We won't announce anything, so we won't have to deal with the press following us and comparing us with the last time they heard the Beatles live."

THE UNIVERSITY TOUR

Rehearsal in London before leaving on the University Tour, 1971. (©1972 MPL Communications Ltd/ Photographer: Robert Ellis. All rights reserved)

On February 8, 1972, McCartney informed the band members they would be leaving the next day on a tour of universities for which they had no scheduled dates. He didn't tell them where they were going or for how long, so Denny threw some t-shirts, jeans and underwear into a bag and the next day he took a cab to McCartney's residence at 7 Cavendish Ave.

"The rest of the band arrived, and Paul said, 'Where's Monique?' I said, 'She's at home. We're going on tour, so she's at home.' He said, 'Call her up. She needs to come along.' He calls her up and says, 'Pack a bag, you need to get up here.' Just like that. He didn't say, 'We need you to watch the kids while we're onstage,' he just said, 'Get up here.'"

Linda had always trusted Monique to watch the kids when she couldn't, even in the home when Rose, the housekeeper, wasn't around. So, Monique

The minimalistic set-up on the first Wings tour. (Photo by Trevor Jones)

packed a bag and the Seiwells' landlord kindly agreed to watch the cat at the very last minute.

"There was a box truck that held the equipment, and we had a 12-passenger transit van. It was the band and Monique, the kids—Heather, Mary, and Stella—and the two dogs: Lucky, the dalmatian, and Martha, the sheepdog. We threw everything in the van. Paul actually drove," Denny says incredulously.

"We got in the van and said, 'Where should we go?' And we started looking at maps and we started driving. We picked out names that looked good. I don't know how we did any of this without cell phones back then and no reservations at hotels, nothing!"

Nottingham University was their first stop. Ian Horne and Trevor Jones in the equipment truck pulled in first and the van followed behind them.

"Ian and Trevor went into the student union and asked, 'Is there someplace we can put on a concert tonight?' And they said, 'I don't know, right now there are finals going on and the students are going to be studying.' And one of them said, 'Well, we've got Paul McCartney out there in the van with his new band.' And they went, 'What?!' So, they came out to look and there was Paul, waving from the van. The first (show) was in the cafeteria. I don't remember if it was during the day or dinnertime, but Ian and Trevor would set up the equipment—the little P.A. that they rented, it was a joke—while we would go around the area looking for a hotel. We stayed in a few no-star hotels. We stayed in some funky places, I tell ya! There was one with a bald little old man who was a night clerk who wasn't very smart—he was one taco short of a combination plate."

Horne and Jones would set up the gear and then put up a few posters that they had made up. "And the kids paid, I think, it was 75 pence and at the time one pound was $1.75, so it was less than that," Denny says.

Then the band would come back to play the gig—despite the fact that they didn't have enough material for an entire show. Seiwell says they would repeat "Give Ireland Back to the Irish," because it was one of only rockers they had, and it allowed them to blow off steam. Denny says the song was received very well on the tour. They mainly did songs from the *Wild Life* album, but no Beatles material. After the show they would get in the van and split up the money.

"We were this happy little family that wasn't connected to the Beatles at all," he says. "We were just a little band out trying to have fun; couldn't wait until

The equipment van and 12-passenger transit van picked them up the day they left on the University Tour. (©1972 MPL Communications Ltd/ Photographer: Robert Ellis. All rights reserved)

the gig was over so we could go to some local hotel and listen to the board mix. The (hotel) room was so small we had to leave the door open while we all sat on the bed with guitars and listened to the night's performance. A night guard came up to Paul one night and handed him a pail and shovel and said, 'One of your dogs just shit in the hallway. Clean it up.' The next day we would wake up and it was, 'Where are we going today?' After about three or four shows, the press started looking for us."

At one little bed and breakfast inn, they ran into a little trouble with the law.

"We woke up in the morning to Heather pounding on the door and saying, 'Dad said for everyone to pack up and get out of here. We have to leave.' Paul had a little argument with the owner of the bed and breakfast, and apparently his elbow hit the guy's nose and (the owner) called the cops and said he was assaulted by Paul McCartney. We jumped into the van and got out of there lickety-split."

Denny believes that's where Paul got the idea for "Band on the Run," although McCartney would not confirm that with him.

Wings did several shows before the press caught on.

Denny says it was not at all difficult traveling with Paul and Linda as a married couple. "They were wonderful together. She was always on his arm. She was his anchor and support. The kids were there with them. They were the best parents I've ever seen. If there wasn't a bed for Stella, Linda would just pull out a drawer and put a pillow in it and that would be Stella's bed. We would stop at a grocery store and Linda would run in and buy a bunch of carrots and hand each one of the kids a carrot. It was really wild when you stop and think of it."

Denny remembers outside the city of Kingston upon Hull, after they had performed at the university on February 11, they stopped at a home that had a fish and chips room in their living room where he had the best fish and chips he's ever had in his life. They'd go to little pubs and have a chip butty sandwich, which was French fries on toast with butter and a pint of beer.

"We weren't getting drunk, although Henry did a little more drinking than we did," Seiwell notes. "We'd celebrate after the show—sometimes, not always—we'd stop at a pub and we'd all have a Scotch and coke, which was the Beatles' drink. Then sometimes we'd stay up all night singing songs and playing guitars. I would get bored with that because I didn't have a guitar and a lot of it was that skiffle music I wasn't familiar with, so I would duck out when I could. But we were just all so family oriented."

Even though it was fairly brief, with the University Tour under their belts, the musicians felt as though they had broken in the band. Not long after the University Tour ended, on February 23, 1972, the group began recording *Red Rose Speedway* in March through June at Olympic Studios. EMI squashed the idea of their desire to put out a double album, feeling it was too early for a new band.

RED ROSE SPEEDWAY

Denny says he loved producer Glyn Johns, who was brought in to helm the project. Seiwell claims he got the best recorded drum sound on him of anyone ever.

"He had a specific method of miking drums with three Sennheiser microphones," Denny says, describing the positioning. "If you picture me

Recording "My Love" at Abbey Road in 1972. (© 1972 Paul McCartney / Photographer: Linda McCartney. Under exclusive license to MPL Archive LLP.)

Vocal overdubs at Abbey Road. (© 1972 Paul McCartney / Photographer: Linda McCartney. Under exclusive license to MPL Archive LLP.)

sitting at the kit, there would be one above my head on my left as far up as my left arm could reach, and then on my right, above the floor tom as far as my right arm could reach there would be another microphone, and then a few feet in front of the bass drum there would be another microphone. He would blend the three of those microphones and it would allow me to play very soft or loud. It sounded so natural. There weren't any studio tricks to improve the sound of the toms or cymbals then, and his method was so simple and made it sound so organic. The first time I heard a playback… oh, man! We had great drum sounds on all of Wings' records, but when Glyn came on the scene, I was just thrilled."

Promo shot for "C Moon" release. Band in gray jumpsuits for visual effect on video. (©1972 MPL Communications Ltd/ Photographer: Barry Lategan. All rights reserved.)

Denny recalls the recording of "C Moon," a track they recorded during that time but was not included on the album (it was released as a double A-side with "Hi, Hi, Hi" in 1972): "We were just fooling around one day, and Henry got behind the drums and I picked up the bass, because Paul was playing piano. I can't play the bass; it buzzes and everything. Henry was playing this drum part that only a non-drummer would think to play, and I'm pretty sure it's the take that's on the record," says Seiwell. McCartney replaced his bass part, but Denny put trumpet and cornet on the track, and played the xylophone part as well. "I bought a little cornet down on Portobello Road at the little flea market and it surprised them when I played it one day in the studio. I recorded trumpet on a couple of songs: 'C Moon' and 'Single Pigeon.'"

Denny remembers recording bits and pieces of songs like "C Moon," "Mama's Girl," the album's final four-song medley: "Hold me Tight," "Lazy Dynamite," "Hands of Love" and "Power Cut."

"Little Lamb Dragonfly" was an unfinished song from the *RAM* period that they worked on once again at Trident Studios in London. "Trident was like EMI: A tall room with an upstairs control room looking down on the studio,

"My Love" video shoot set in London. (©1973 MPL Communications Ltd/ Photographer: Sheila Rock.))

I believe. Paul was in there fooling around on an upright piano with 'Little Lamb Dragonfly' and said he wanted to finish it. I offered my help and said, 'Well, why don't we do this?' and I came up with some parts for background vocals on a section he needed to finish, and he said, 'That's good!' So, we got the band together and got around the microphone. I showed everyone their parts and we started singing the background vocals."

In 2012 Denny revisited the memorable staircase in Abbey Road Studio 2 he went up and down so many times from the recording studio to the control room. (Photo by Monique Seiwell)

"Get on the Right Thing" was a track they also started during the *RAM* era, as well as "I Lie Around," which ended up on a special edition of the album. "'I Lie Around' is really one of those very special McCartney songs," Denny remarks. "The writing, the recording, the whole thing."

Seiwell recalls that McCartney wanted a danceable, disco vibe on "Night Out." "What we came up with was a no-brainer, but I didn't really think it was really worthy of what the band was capable of making," Seiwell admits of the track included on the special edition.

He says "Loup (1st Indian on the Moon)" started out with a lot of tom toms to make it sound like an American Indian song.

THE OTHER SIDE OF THE COIN

Lee Eastman, Linda's father, was a powerful attorney, and also McCartney's choice to represent the Beatles in their final days together. McCartney was outvoted 3-1 in this matter by the other Beatles, and their attorney became Allen Klein. Eastman did, however, manage McCartney's solo career, and in March, 1972, he held a meeting with Wings up at the McCartney house.

"We were all up at the house and we were having a meeting with Lee, and he said, 'Okay, this is how the financial thing is going to work with the band...' He was trying to help us set up some kind of agreement and we were all looking forward to what he had to say. Unfortunately, he said that in checking into everything, that Denny Laine had an agreement with his manager, Tony Secunda, and it was such a bad agreement that it would affect all of us. Unless he could get Denny Laine out of this agreement with his manager, he couldn't go ahead and move forward to put together an agreement for Wings."

They inherited a lot of baggage, from the Beatles break-up and the individual members that came into Wings.

"They were the best and worst times. Here we were, breaking in a new band on the coattails of the biggest band to ever to exist in history, yet we had these insurmountable problems that we didn't even know about. Paul kept a lot of (those things) hush-hush, under the table and didn't bring them in and wasn't open about them. He didn't tell us what was going on, and we just tried to stay positive and keep doing what we were doing."

WINGS OVER EUROPE TOUR

Before leaving on their Wings Over Europe Tour, the Seiwells moved from Draycott Place to a small row house on Alderville Road. The tour began on July

At Emerson, Lake & Palmer's rehearsal studio rehearsing for the European tour. (Photo by Trevor Jones)

9, 1972, and the band met their open-topped, double-decker hippie painted bus in Ollioules, France, where they played their first show at Chateauvallon.

"That first night, Linda started crying on my shoulder. She was scared. I said, 'It's a little late for that now,'" Denny recalls. "She hadn't played in front of people for a while, and she was petrified. I said, 'we're going out there.'"

Denny celebrated his birthday the next day (July 10) on the bus making their way to Antibes for their next gig.

"The bus wasn't super comfortable," he says. "The top deck was open for sunbathing in the south of France. There were mattresses, so while it wasn't that comfortable, it was fun."

On his birthday, Denny recalls going to a posh outdoor disco on the beach in the south of France. He says the band acted like "fools," he got hammered and fell into the fountain.

Seiwell recalls staying at the Hotel du Cap-Eden-Roc, one of the most exclusive hotels in the world, for several days. At the time, the hotel only accepted payment in cash (a policy they only changed in 2006). Denny says later he and McCartney joked about the $30 hard-boiled egg.

"That is probably one of the reasons we didn't make any money on the tour,"

Hotel du Cap-Eden-Roc at Cap d'Antibes, 1972. (Photo by Monique Seiwell)

At the gig in Antibes in the South of France on Denny's birthday July 10, 1972. (Photo by Monique Seiwell.)

Seiwell surmises. "We didn't just stay in hotels. Sometimes we'd stay in castles like in Germany and Denmark. I remember one morning asking the baron what he could make for breakfast."

They arrived at Hotel du Cap-Eden-Roc at 5:00 a.m., unshowered and sweaty from the gig the night before and very road-tired after being on the bus (which only went 35 miles per hour). They had asked the hotel to have breakfast ready for them when they arrived, and when they got there, they were ushered into a large room filled with antiques and a buffet spread before them.

"There was a huge loup de mer, a type of fish—it had to be three feet long—and all these little canapes and all this fancy French food, and all (the band) wanted was a bangers and mash—a British breakfast. There's this dead fish on a mirrored platter and the band is going, 'What the fuck is this?' But the place was so gorgeous!"

While staying at the hotel, they rented a couple of cars, and McCartney offered the Seiwells a car to take to Nice, which was close by, to see Monique's family. They knew the area well, so they took the red convertible and hit the road.

First day on the bus, South of France 1972. (©1972 MPL Communications Ltd. All rights reserved.)

Top deck of the bus, stuffed with mattresses and pillows perfect for sunbathing, South of France. (Photo by Monique Seiwell)

"We put the top down to enjoy the south of France and when we closed it, somehow she got her finger caught in the mechanics and it put a big gash in it," Denny recalls. "We had to go see a doctor; she had a horrible big bandage on her hand and a big rubber finger on her middle finger."

Their set-up was bare bones compared to what it became later on the tour, Seiwell explains. On later dates, the Stones' 16-track mobile truck recorded the performances, and in the bigger venues, they had a 70mm screen with two drive-in theater projectors showing films behind the band on stage.

"We went from nothing to everything, and we had a crew of close to 60 people," he recalls.

Denny's red platform boots he bought in Paris were too small, but he wore them anyway, and after France, they departed for Germany, where they stayed in castles. Seiwell says they may not have made money, but they saw Europe like nobody but someone touring with Paul McCartney could see it.

After Germany, they traveled on to Switzerland. At the Pavilion Montreux show in Switzerland, Seiwell recalls, for some reason, Linda had a sour look

Backstage on the European tour in Germany. (Photo by Trevor Jones)

on her face. She seemed miserable.

"We went to a restaurant afterwards and Anita Pallenberg ('60s actress/model) was there. We were upstairs eating fondue and throwing it on the accordion player downstairs (we were drunk), and Henry said to Linda, right in front of Paul, "If I have to look over at that fuckin' hatchet-face of yours one more time while we're trying to perform…"

After that, McCullough called McCartney and threatened to leave the band. He was pretty much unhappy with everything.

Luckily the band had a two-week break after Montreux, and they returned to the road on August 1 in Copenhagen, Denmark with the mobile truck to record the shows and a larger crew. Shortly after they had gotten back on tour, in Helsinki, Finland, Seiwell took his one and only acid trip with a couple of other band members. They were staying in a beautiful hotel on a lake with small boats docked, as Seiwell recalls.

"That same night some folk singer had given us a lump of hash that had white veins running through it, and we smoked this opiated hash. Everybody got

Photo of the full band at soundcheck before the Tivoli Gardens concert in August 1972.(Photo by Monique Seiwell)

Paul and Linda goofing around at soundcheck at Tivoli Gardens in Copenhagen, August 1972. (Photo by Monique Seiwell)

up at 3:00 in the morning and went downstairs to look for food. One by one we were walking into the lobby looking for food, laughing our asses off. That's when we took the acid. We were hanging out, walking down these little docks where they had these little boats. It was very tame, but memorable. Another night on the road. It was just, 'Look at that, look at that.'"

BUSTED!

About a week and half later, they all began to complain that they didn't have weed. There had been some bits and pieces along the way, but there was nothing substantial.

"There were a couple of guys in London who had weed, so I made a call to someone in London and asked them to drop off some weed to the office and they would get it to us," Seiwell recounts. "It was five or six ounces of African weed, and they wrapped it up and put it in the mail. They wrapped paper around it with string and. (The package) said 'cassettes,' and it was soft like a bunch of socks. This guy in the office put my name on it. It was caught by customs before it left London, and they contacted the authorities in Gothenburg (Sweden) where it was addressed to the hotel there. We were on the bus, and the office had told Paul and Linda that some weed was coming to the hotel. The band went to the venue to do a soundcheck, but when we got to the edge of the city, a limo met the bus, and (Paul and Linda) jumped in to go to the hotel to try to get the weed. And that's what implicated them."

The McCartneys proceeded to the venue, a giant arena called the Scandinavium. After informing the band that the weed had not arrived, they commenced with soundcheck and then the show. At the end of the performance, they went into an extra encore when the P.A. suddenly stopped working. What they didn't realize was that the additional song had messed up the timing for the police bust that was about to take place.

"They descended upon us. We were onstage, we finished the tune and the cops came onstage. I've got my little outfit on—my sequined jacket—and they take me offstage first because my name was on the package. They grab me on each side and walk me off the stage after the last tune. Because we did the extra song, they chopped the 20,000-watt P.A. cable. It could have fried the guy that did it, but that's how we knew something was going on. They took me offstage and the rest of the band went back to the dressing room. I'm sitting in the room at the cop shop and then I hear Paul and Linda, screaming down the hallway. I'm in one room and they're in another room. The cops were really nice, apologizing that they can't give us a sandwich or a drink or even a towel—we're all so sweaty because we just got offstage.

"I'm alone in a room with a cop and then the promoter, John Morris, shows up with the money to pay it off. He gave them $1,200 *each* and we went back to the hotel. As we're leaving the cop shop, the press is out front and they're taking pictures and the next morning the headline was KNARK SMUGGLE."

As the large tour crew saw the bust going down at the concert venue, they all grabbed their weed and gave it to Ian Horne. In the concert hall was a raised platform with the mixing board; Horne took all the dope and shoved it under a rug beneath the mixing board. He did not want to take it back to the hotel in fear that the cops would be there—and it was a smart move, because they were.

"They came to our rooms, and they were looking through our rooms for drugs," Seiwell says. "At that point it was getting nasty. Ian told the police, 'I'm in charge of our equipment. I have to go back to the venue and make sure it's all stowed away properly.' Ian gets a cop car to get him to take him back to the venue and he gets everybody's dope from under the rug, shoves it down his pants, gets back into the cop car and comes back to the hotel, and we partied."

The next morning a famous hippie from Amsterdam showed up in Gothenburg. The band was on the bus, getting ready to go to the next gig, and he brought them a pound of marijuana. With the press all over them, they drew the curtains, and as Denny describes it, everyone had a little paper plate, and they were cleaning seeds out of the pot.

There was definitely some fallout from the Gothenburg bust. McCartney didn't know that it would keep him from touring the States for three years, so unfortunately, he lost millions in revenue and the worst of it for Denny was the pain it caused his parents. For two days he ruminated about the phone call he knew he had to make. After all, it was international news, and he knew his parents must have heard about it back in Pennsylvania.

Sure enough, when he finally got the courage to call, "My mom said, 'Why didn't you just kill us? Why didn't you just stab us in the heart?' They really took it in the worst way. We were a churchgoing family and drugs just didn't fly. In fact, the night before, they had gone to the farmer's market in the country, outside the little town we lived in. They were walking around and there was an announcement on the public address system: 'Local boy Denny Seiwell gets busted with Beatle in Sweden with marijuana.' My parents just wanted to shrink away. It was just terrible. I said, 'Look Mom, I'm the same kid you raised. It's no big deal.' I calmed them down, but that was really hard to do. My mother was crying."

The band continued to the next gig via ferry, along with their weed. When the ferry reached the other side, there were policemen all around on the dock.

"The crew's bus and our bus were on the ferry. The crew had been rolling joints the whole tour. As you roll a hash joint, little bits and crumples fall out, and it's all over the floorboard, and the same with our bus. And we said, 'Oh fuck, they're going to nail us again. This is going to turn into a real megillah!' They had dogs and they ran them through the buses, and they didn't find anything. We walked down the dock; we had been rolling joints and we stuck our fingers and our hands in front of the dogs and the dogs didn't smell anything on us either. We got into the bus and went to the next gig. But it was harrowing."

Before the next show, a British journalist named Paul Dacre came to their hotel, telling them he was there to do a story on how the band was one big happy family, traveling around Europe doing concerts. They'd soon find out he was lying.

"Paul remembered that this guy's father had done a story on the Beatles, so he let him come along to soundcheck that day. He said he was not there to review the band or to cover the bust or anything but just get some info on how we lived on the road. Paul thought that was a good angle, considering what had just happened. So (Dacre) came to the soundcheck, he heard half of it, flew back to London and wrote the article. A couple of days later, we got a copy of the article, and he had given a complete review of the concert (despite) not having been there—and not a good one. He did exactly what he said he wasn't going to do. There was nothing about how we traveled as a family. There was drug stuff in there about the bust; everything he said he wasn't going to do, he did. This really upset Paul and Linda."

When they got back to the hotel, Paul and Linda took one of the little Queen Elizabeth plastic soap dishes from their bathroom and took one of baby Stella's poops, wrapped it up and sent it to Dacre.

At an old hotel in Rotterdam, as they checked in, they were told there were ghosts in the hotel.

"The rooms were beautiful and everything, but in the middle of the night we start hearing some funny shit: creaking, doors opening and stuff," says Denny. "Heather, who was 10 or 11 years old at the time, had a nice imagination, and she started pulling some shit in the middle of the night like she was a ghost, going around to different people's rooms. It was cute as hell."

In Amsterdam they played the Concertgebouw, which Seiwell compares to playing the prestigious Carnegie Hall in the United States.

"We stayed in a beautiful old hotel right on one of the canals called the Pulitzer. It was everything and then some," Denny says. "Playing that venue and staying in that hotel was very memorable. We walked around the streets of Amsterdam and ate those little puff pastries that the street vendors made, and we had a marvelous time. And I'm sure there was some dope smoked there. We were on the move, so I'm sure there wasn't a lot of time for frivolity."

They had to fly to the last two dates in Belgium and West Germany.

"The bus went 35 miles an hour, so it would take forever to get anywhere," Denny says. "Occasionally we were going to be late for the concert. We were on the motorway and all of a sudden five lime green BMWs showed up. We all piled into these cars and went 135 miles per hour to make it to the gig in time, and the bus came later on to pick us up after the gig. A couple of times we had to do that, and a couple of times we had to fly."

During the final gigs, they stayed at another very exclusive hotel on the main square of Berlin with war monuments all around it.

"If you looked out the window, there was a building that had been kept

Backstage during the European tour. (©1972 MPL Communications Ltd/ Photographer: Joe 'Captain Snap' Steven. All rights reserved)

intact after the war that had not been reconstructed, so it was a memory of the war. That night, for some reason or another, Niq and I had our biggest fight. She said, 'I'm never doing this again!' She wanted to go on the road, but after doing a whole tour, she said, 'I'll never do this again.' It's hard and it wears everyone's nerves to a fray. Paul and Linda were in the next room, and we were standing toe to toe, screaming at each other, and they were hearing it all. It freaked them out. That night we did our final show at the Deutschlandhalle. At the end of the show, a lot of confetti and balloons were dropped. And Niq was holding a couple of Paul and Linda's kids out in the melee of all that chaos, and she had a ring that her grandmother had given her with a living stone that would change colors over time. The stone fell out of the ring and she noticed it in all of the madness."

With all the confetti and balloons on the floor, as the hall emptied out, the entire crew was on their hands and knees searching for the stone through the mess, to no avail. They all returned to the hotel, then piled into a Mercedes cab to attend the afterparty. Denny says he thinks there were seven in the cab when the police pulled them over.

"They saw it was Paul McCartney, and they didn't care. They said there were too many people in the cab, and we had to get out. I don't remember what happened; we may have walked the rest of the way."

That ended the tour. They took a private jet back to London. Upon their return, there was a fleet of lawyers waiting for them to get them through customs just in case there was any problem because of the bust that had occurred in Sweden, and because Linda and Denny were Americans and they might not allow them back into the country.

"We were whisked through customs. They never opened a bag; they stamped my passport—good for another year. It was amazing. We were home before we knew it."

Everyone had a little time off. Denny and Monique took a vacation to New York. McCartney called them back early to go into the studio and some personal chaos met the Seiwells. Shortly after their return from New York to their home on Alderville Road, the owner of their rental, Colonel Metcalfe, the head of the British Women's Army, showed up at their house. They had only lived here for a few months, but she had heard about the bust on the tour and said, "In order for you to stay in my house and continue renting it, you're going to have to sign a document stating there will be no drugs used on the premises on my property."

"We're leaving," they said, and regretfully packed up.

"It was such a cute place," says Denny. "It had a cleaning lady from Soho and an Irish gardener named Peter who would come once a week to cut the grass and tend to the roses in the little garden in the back. He wore an old black suit and hat, and he had a newspaper under his arm. He was paid 75 pence for his duties, which was something like $1.75. He was very sweet. He'd take his hat off, and when we became his bosses, his pay went up from 75 pence to a whole pound. I would pour him a big glass of scotch and I'd put the glass of scotch on top of the pound note; he'd see that and his eyes would light up. I'd say, 'Go ahead,' so he would knock back the shot of scotch and he'd go do his job. I'd refill the glass and put it on top of the pound. He'd finish his job, come back and knock back the second shot, put the quid in his pocket, and I'm sure he went straight off to the pub. He was a very sweet, old gentleman. It was really a drag to have to leave that house."

They found a one-bedroom, furnished basement apartment on Sydney Place in South Kensington.

"There was a tiny little bathroom that had a toilet with a tank at the top and a chain with a handle on it above that you pulled to flush the toilet," he remembers. "The name on that tank was Thomas Crapper and Sons."

Back at work at Morgan Studios, Seiwell recalls one day standing outside with McCartney and a beautiful Bentley S3 pulled up. It was completely white: white wall tires, white leather interior, white fur rugs inside.

"It's old, classic, pristine," Denny says. "And inside is a guy dressed in all white, with white hair. He got out of the car, and it was Alan White from Yes. Paul and I looked at one another and said, 'Now that's what a rock star looks like.' And Alan and I were friends from that day on, until he recently passed away."

Their finances were still very much in disarray. Seiwell was putting everything onto his American Express card. He would have his residual checks sent to his father in Pennsylvania and his father would deposit them into a bank account and pay the bills that came to his address. Denny trusted that the royalty money would come as promised, but after playing 28 cities to packed venues on a sold-out concert tour it was hard to believe it when McCartney came to them and said, "I just got the word from John Morris that we spent so much on expenses that we're in the hole for the tour."

"We were living in this funky little apartment, and it was next to Kings Road, which was very festive at the time during the hippie movement. We were in the center of it all even though it wasn't much of an apartment. It was in a good location. And we had a phone and a car—a 1964 Mercedes 230SL two-seater with a hardtop and a soft top."

"LIVE AND LET DIE"

One day Paul called the band to the house, and they drove up there to find that Horne and Jones had set up their equipment in the McCartney living room.

"Paul says, 'I've just been asked to write the theme for the new Bond movie. They sent me the book, the new Ian Fleming novel which I read the other night, so I'm going to start writing this Bond theme.' He goes over to the piano and we're just sitting there watching this. He goes, 'Okay, James Bond, chase scenes.'"

The way Denny describes it, McCartney just launched into the dynamic chase scene that catapults the song after the piano opening. Seiwell says he worked on that for a minute and then double-backed to the little love scene that opens the song, which just poured out.

"He said, 'Because it takes place in Jamaica, we have to get some reggae in there.' We all loved that kind of music and had already done some of it on other songs, so we did the little reggae section. He literally wrote the song in 15-20 minutes. We were sitting there amazed; my jaw was on the floor. We went over to our instruments and started working it out. Denny Laine played bass, Paul played piano, Henry played guitar, I played drums, and we started knocking it into shape. Within an hour or two, we had our parts for the different movements for the song. I think he had a two-track in his living room, and he ran a tape of one of the rehearsals. After we were happy with the arrangement for what we came up with, he recorded it and sent it to George Martin. It was rough, but George wrote the orchestrations and there was a full-on orchestra. As I recall, it had to be done fairly quickly, and we were up at AIR Studios London within the week and there was a small orchestra in the big room. There was a big room and a back room. The big room was more for film and scoring dates. You could put a 40-60-piece orchestra in there pretty easily and I remember the sound was amazing because the floor did not touch the walls. That was one of the highlights of George's studio. So the sound was amazing when you put an orchestra in there."

For the October 1972 "Live and Let Die" recording session the orchestra was scattered throughout the room. Denny went into a partially enclosed drum booth. McCartney played piano, Denny Laine played bass and is actually listed as the bass player on the track. Henry played guitar, Linda added some keyboards and background vocals, and Ray Cooper played some percussion. Seiwell says they only did around four or five takes, and that McCartney sang live.

"We were in and out of there in less than three hours. It takes most bands that much time to get a drum sound," Seiwell says with a laugh.

The crazy result was when they sent the finished product to the film producers, Albert "Cubby" Broccoli wanted to know if it was the demo.

"Paul stuck to his guns. Take it or leave it. Paul could be pretty tough," Denny attests.

It was the first rock song to appear in a Bond movie and the first to be nominated for an Academy Award, although it lost out to Alan and Marilyn Bergman/Marvin Hamlisch's "The Way We Were."

In hindsight, Seiwell is not surprised at Broccoli's stunning reaction. Many years later, while Denny was writing his 2015 drum book *What Not to Play! A Drummer's Guide to Crafting a Drum Part* for Alfred Music, he intended to include instruction on "Live and Let Die." He received permission from McCartney and Sony, but Broccoli would not sign off.

"JAMES PAUL MCCARTNEY" SPECIAL

"Live and Let Die" debuted on a TV special called "James Paul McCartney," airing on April 16, 1973 in the U.S. and May 10 in the U.K. (The *Live and Let Die* film itself did not premiere in the U.S. until June 27.) "Live and Let Die" immediately became the most favored Bond song ever heard. To this day, it contends with Adele's "Skyfall."

The band had gone to Marrakesh, Morroco in February of 1973 to rehearse for the special. They stayed at the Mamounia Hotel for about a week, and Denny says he doesn't recall getting a lot of rehearsal done.

"I remember going to the marketplace and the local drummers were banging on their drums, wearing their white robes and dancing; it was quite amazing. We took carriage rides into exotic gardens. One day we were in the marketplace in the center square. And one day I was in the marketplace with Paul and some guy came up to us and said, 'Do you want to buy some hashish?' He said, 'Follow me, I'll take you.' Paul said, 'You want to do this?' I said, 'Yeah, come on, let's go.' Paul and I are following this guy and we're back into the little city with these tiny little walkways and apartments. We follow the guy into his apartment, he gets the hash out and gives us a little bit. We tried it out and it wasn't very good. By this time, we were both a little nervous about getting out of there alive because we were out in the ghetto, so he looked at me and I looked at him and I said, 'It's crap,' but just to get out of there alive, he bought some anyway. It was total crap, but we made it out of there and got back to the hotel. We had little bits and pieces we found here and there. There was supposed to be a dealer named Abdul that hung out in the hotel disco."

One night they were down by the disco looking for Abdul. Denny spotted him and called out his name. He said, "Yes? You want something?" Denny Laine and Seiwell took Abdul back to Seiwell's room where there was a beautiful large Moroccan brass coffee table in the center of the living room. They rolled some joints to test out Abdul's hash, and when they asked him the price, Abdul got offended.

"We said, 'It's not that good,' and the guy started to get a little antsy. He said, 'You know I've got a gun in my pocket.' We were pretty lit from drinking and there was a bottle of Courvoisier on this ornate table. When (Abdul) said the thing about the gun, Denny picked up this bottle of Courvoisier and he was going to break it and threaten the guy with it. He banged it on the table, but it didn't break. It was a pint of Courvoisier in a plastic bottle. Denny wanted to play the big man, but I'm watching this and laughing my ass off. I don't know how we got out of that, but we got the guy out of the room, and we never saw him again."

Then there was the day a rich American woman invited the whole band to dinner. She lived with a baron and obviously enjoyed the local customs. Monique was there, as well as McCullough's wife Sheila and Laine's wife Jo Jo.

"They had hired drummers and dancers from the square to come and entertain us. We were smoking and sitting on the pillows like you do in Morocco and all of a sudden, these guys bust in and start slamming drums and dancing around. We're having a great ol' time. And then they bring in the lamb that's going to be our dinner to meet us. They walk him in. That was just terrible because Paul and Linda had that farm with the sheep. Yeah, that wasn't good. I think they probably were completely vegetarian already. And the lamb is going, 'Bah, bah.'"

At the marketplace, they designed their own Moroccan tops; they picked the fabric, the stitching and colors. In one shop, there were Moroccan rugs. There was one Denny admired and on the first day he asked its price. The owner told him 250 British pounds. He replied it was too much. He would pass by every day and inquire and the owner would come down in price a little each time. Denny finally got him down to 50 quid and Denny grabbed the rug, which the band used one day in a photo shoot in the desert with a camel.

"There's a great picture of us in our kaftans sitting on the rug holding clay instruments that we bought as souvenirs while we were there."

Two days after they returned to London, they began working on the special at ATV (Associated Television) which was the original name of the British

Denny doing the tourist thing and riding a camel in Morocco. (Photo by Monique Seiwell)

broadcaster, part of Britain's Independent Television network (ITV). Gary Smith and Dwight Hemion produced the 50-minute show, which had a variety of segments.

"They built a set for us, and we did several things live. They brought in a live audience for some of it," he recalls. "There were a couple hundred young kids, and the set was built with huge streams of mylar like mirrors which went from floor to ceiling which gave it an expansive look. It really looked good on camera. I had a Nudie shirt with a cowboy setting, with a saddle and corral for one segment."

Denny teases that the closing piece, "Live and Let Die" nearly did kill some of the players in the orchestra. They hadn't been told how the piano Paul was playing was rigged to break in half and blow up at the final chords. Of course there could only be one take, so they had to get it right.

"And here are these old violin players who don't know anything, and they are sitting there with their Stradivariuses and their wigs on. We get to the very end of the song and there's a guy up in the rafters who pushes a button, and the piano blows up. Well, the charge is a little bit bigger than they thought it was going to be, and when it blew up, Henry was eight feet to the left of Paul, and Linda was to the left of him and the blast swept Henry off his feet. I was ducking in behind my cymbals because I knew it was coming. The piano lid was made of balsa wood and it blew up in a ball of flames. It went up and over these violin players' heads. I'm surprised one of them didn't have a heart attack. They didn't know it was coming; the piano broke in half and from the angle they shot Paul, it looked like he was playing the piano, but he was actually about three feet back from it. They actually did a great job on it."

Seiwell says the day they shot "Mary Had a Little Lamb" in the park, a lot of fun was had.

"There was a tree and a swing and there was footage of us out on a boat in a lake. On a break we played a little soccer, and I remember I was playing a little too rough for everyone because I was playing American-style football and I was bigger than everyone, too. It was all in good fun. But then they had us set up by a little tree and we were going to film 'Mary Had a Little Lamb' with a herd of sheep. We had to be very quiet because of this herd of sheep and we were all looking at one another like, 'Who's going to screw this up?' I figured it would be Henry, but I tapped the bass drum, and the sheep went flying like crazy. They had to start all over again and round them up, and that happened a few times. Even Paul was laughing. Then he had to sit down and pretend he was singing to 'Mary Had a Little Lamb,' and even the slightest movement, the sheep would freak and scatter. You can hear them baaa-ing in the background and it's very cute."

They went to a pub on the Mersey for the special with several of McCartney's family members. Denny says there was no performance; just a gathering of family where they drank a little too much, which he says went on a bit too long.

"So, Henry, Denny and I get back in the limo to go back to London, and the driver pulls away and he stops for a second, rolls down the window and throws up because he's drunk, too. I say to him, 'Wait a minute, you can't drive us if you're drunk. I'm driving.' He moved over and I got in the driver's seat and drove the limo; I was probably the least drunk of everyone. Denny and Henry were in the back seat, really loaded. They started arguing and putting cigarettes out on each other and all sorts of crazy stuff. It was a nightmare ride, and I'm surprised we made it back without a major episode. It was definitely a memorable night."

MICE AND FROGS

Even before "Live and Let Die" was recorded, McCartney began filming *The Bruce McMouse Show* at Elstree Studios. The idea in 1972 was part concert footage and part animation about a family of Mice living below the stage where Wings performs. Animator Eric Wylam based the final characters on original sketches that McCartney created, and Paul and Linda did some of the voice-overs. The project was shelved, unfinished, in the late '70s, but restored and released in 2018.

As Denny describes the family of mice, he says the cartoon mouse father, Bruce, who had a mustache, would interact with the band.

"It was that corny stuff that McCartney really enjoyed doing," Seiwell says, mentioning the 13-minute animated film McCartney released in 1984 called *Rupert and the Frog Song,* which included music from the days he was in Wings.

Speaking to the imaginary mouse in the Bruce McMouse Show was a difficult task.

"Delivering lines to an imaginary mouse in the palm of my hand was very hard," Denny says, "The director was saying, 'That's good, keep doing it, repeat it.' I wasn't an actor, and I had no tools. But the fun day was the day they had to film Linda. That was probably the only time Linda was away from Paul. She was always on his arm and around him. So, Paul was back with us in a little room just hanging out with us and that day he told us some stories about the Beatles days that he never (told us before). Stories about after the shows and what it was like for them and all the girls, and it was just us guys talking. It was the only time we saw Paul as one of the guys. It was just a moment when he was a regular guy, just one of us. It was a real bonding moment, and we just loved him a whole lot more."

After Wings filmed the special, they performed on the perfunctory British TV shows of the day, like *Top of the Pops* and *The Old Grey Whistle Test,* with clothing they had designed. One appearance Denny recalls was in a gray painter's overalls with shoulder straps, which they wore uniformly on a set with a gray piano.

THE U.K. TOUR

Early in 1973, Emerson, Lake & Palmer, the English progressive supergroup made up of Keith Emerson, Greg Lake and Carl Palmer, bought an abandoned movie theater in Fulham, London. They stripped it of all the seats and made it into a rehearsal hall.

"Paul heard about this place, and we rented that for a while to rehearse for the U.K. tour. It was right down the street from where we were living, and we would rehearse in this old theater."

Red Rose Speedway came out on Apple on May 4, 1973. Denny says the fact that it had started out as a double album and cut to a single disc made it a bit disjointed. Shortly after its release, Wings left on its U.K. tour.

"By now, the band had become a band. We had paid our dues with the other tours and the special and TV performances and now we were really a band," Seiwell declares. "We played all the places we played on the University Tour, but in big concert halls with good sound equipment and a great P.A."

And cool clothes. Harkening back to Beatle days, McCartney had U.S. go-to fashion designer Dougie Millings create gray suits with lightning bolts on the lapels and tight black pants with a short-sleeved waiter's jacket with sequined lapels.

"I'll never forget going over to Dougie Millings' place, which was across the street from Apple. He had his tailor shop there and upstairs was his office with all his samples and his work. He had a piano in there; he was a songwriter. And when you'd go in for a fitting, he'd play you a song he was just working on. They were cute old British skiffle kind of songs."

On this tour, they had the bus the British soccer team used the year they won the World Cup final. It was an ordinary bus with the seats removed, so there were two seats facing another two seats with a table in the middle.

"It wasn't a tour bus like today, that you could sleep on. We never had anything that was really comfortable, come to think of it," Denny ponders with a laugh. "Sometimes we'd just take the private jet to get someplace and have the bus pick us up from there."

The day of their fourth show in Bournemouth, Seiwell recalls going horseback riding.

"The riding stables were right across the street from the hotel, and everyone hopped on a horse. My horse knew he had an asshole on his back, and he just put his head down and started eating. I couldn't get him to go," Denny recalls with a laugh.

Another memorable stop was three-quarters of the way into the tour, in Glasgow, Scotland, at Green's Playhouse, they put chicken wire in front of the stage, because if the audience didn't like you, they threw beer bottles at you.

"We were leaving the theater, and they had the limo parked outside the door in the alley alongside the theater, keeping the fans out of the alley. We got in the limo, and (fans) burst through the police lines. They were climbing all over the car, so much so that we were afraid that the car would collapse. We were on the floor with our feet on the ceiling. It was kind of weird and kind of scary. It was like the Beatles days."

There was another show where Seiwell doesn't recall the venue, but the theater was upstairs, and the audience was rocking so hard that authorities were fearful that the floor might collapse.

"We had really become a good band," Denny comments.

After the last of three dates at the Hammersmith Odeon, on May 27, 1973, Wings hosted a party at Café Royale, and a who's-who of rock 'n' roll showed up.

"That night Ronnie Wood and I were in the men's room half the time doing things we shouldn't be doing," Denny admits. "Michael Des Barres was there, too. He was the lead singer for a band called Silverhead. He was a friend of Henry's. We were in the bathroom chopping out lines and girls were coming in and out of the men's room, and this little guy in his little Café Royale outfit comes in and says, 'Oh, there are girls in the men's room,' and he taps Michael on the shoulder and says, 'Miss, you're not allowed…' and Michael turns around and says, 'I'm no fuckin' miss.' I guess from the back he looked like a woman."

Denny says it was a rare night for a very straight-laced family affair band. "We were usually very tame. Linda was there and the wives were there. While other bands were throwing shit out of the hotel rooms, we were a family unit."

McCartney, Linda, and children on tour bus during U.K. Tour, 1973. (© 1972 MPI Communications ltd/ Photographer: Joe 'Captain Snap' Steven. All rights reserved)

The band took a break for a month. The Seiwells went to the States on vacation. Wings resumed the tour on July 4 in Sheffield for four more dates.

The band was having dinner in their hotel in Birmingham the next evening when, just like "Power Cut" (the song on *Red Rose Speedway*), the electricity went out in the restaurant. Recording artist Jose Feliciano, who was blind, was also dining there. "I recall him getting up and telling us, 'Don't worry fellas, I'll take you back to your rooms. I'm good at this,'" recalls Denny. "It was a beautiful old hotel, and they had candles when the lights would go out."

The tour concluded after the show at the Newcastle City Hall on Denny's birthday, July 10, 1973. On the 27th, the band went to Scotland to prepare for the *Band on the Run* rehearsals, which began on July 31.

THE BEGINNING OF THE END

Wings had just done a major tour of Britain. The musicians saw it as successful and yet there was no money. As they began rehearsing the new material, morale was low.

"Here we were rehearsing in Scotland, it was going to be 'go, go, go' and be at the beck and call of the McCartneys and not see any money, still living on 70 quid a week. I don't know how we did it. We'd get little bonuses here and there, but they were small," says Seiwell, explaining they would use the bonus to pay off the bills and immediately go into arrears again.

"We were in the trenches to put him back on the map. We were the only band to come out of the Beatles. We paid with our blood, sweat and tears."

McCartney never noticed. He was managing his world: dealing with the Apple court case and overseeing the building of a studio in Lagos, Nigeria in which to record his next album. While finances were an issue, it wasn't the whole issue. It was the stress, the wear and tear—and the falsehood that Wings was a band. While early on, McCartney had promised a democracy, it was clearly his band and his decisions. There was nothing shared about it—not financially, anyway.

Denny recalls that McCullough was probably staying at the Seiwells while they were in Scotland. Laine, who he describes as a gypsy, might have been camping out on the Low Ranachan property during the recording, and Denny and McCullough would ride over from the Seiwell farm while McCartney might have even ridden a horse over the hill from his main house down to the session.

They'd get in the barn, have a cup of tea and work for hours. Denny believes there was a two-track recorder running in the barn at Low Ranachan when an argument erupted as McCartney told McCullough that he needed to play the solo on "My Love" the same way each time because the fans expected it.

Denny says Paul probably didn't say it in the way it should have been said and McCullough walked out—for good.

It was a big blow to McCartney. He called off rehearsals and the Seiwells went back to London, not knowing if there was a band or not. Denny kept in touch with McCartney, waiting for word on what was to be. Throughout this entire time, in the privacy of their own home, Denny and Monique had conversations about the disappointment. Ultimately, Monique left all the decision making to her husband and told him she would support any decision he made going forward.

The "straw that broke the camel's back" for Seiwell was McCartney's lack of musical respect to the band into which Denny had poured his heart and soul. Seiwell had phoned McCartney in Scotland several times asking if they could postpone the album until they could break in a new guitar player.

"We'd become a band, so to go and do it without Henry seemed so pointless," Denny says. "Paul said, 'No, we'll just do it like *Ram*, we'll just do overdubs.' After working as hard as we had worked and to have sacrificed what we had sacrificed just didn't make sense to do the album this way. 'Couldn't we just find another guitar player to learn Henry's parts and attack this thing like a band?'" But McCartney refused.

Denny felt disposable and dispensable. Today he says he knows McCartney and he had a musical connection; it's obvious in the music they made, but those feelings were very real at the time, and they propelled him to pick up the phone and say, "I'm sorry Paul, I just can't do this anymore. I'm done."

"He was blown away when I said that and he slammed down the phone," Denny recalls. "He was pissed. He could tell I was hurt, but he didn't know how to respond because I think he knew it was true."

And then the phone began to ring. Denny will never forget the first call from Linda: "How dare you inconvenience us!"

He got calls from Mike McGear, Paul's brother and Vincent Romeo, Paul's manager. He did not hear from Paul again.

Looking back, Denny says Paul and Linda came from different worlds from him and Monique. Paul was coming from the Beatles, the top of the world, but Denny says that sometimes he would catch a glimpse of the sweet, down-to-earth Liverpudlian boy, which made him believe that Paul could relate to the plight of those whose needs were different than his. But life experiences do change a person.

"I really regret that I didn't sit him down and say, 'Come on, Paul, we started this thing together and you made me a promise. I know you have problems going on with the Beatles receivership and all that, but we have to do something, some sort of letter of agreement, at least something in writing, about what my compensation for all this work is going to be," Seiwell reflects. "I'm sorry that never occurred, but I was probably afraid to do it. As close as we were, he might have said, 'Well, that's just the way it is right now, if you can't handle it, we'll just get somebody else,' and that was in the back of my mind. And playing with a genius like that, it would just go away."

Ultimately it did go away, and they put out a press release stating that Seiwell departed the band due to musical differences.

THE AFTERMATH

Seiwell did not have one minute of regret in leaving. He was done. He left on August 30 and on September 6 he received a call from producer/manager Andrew Oldham to work on Donovan's *Essence to Essence.* He also did a record with Don Preston from Leon Russell's band at Apple Records, with whom he would work later in the U.S.

In retrospect, he realizes he was hoping that McCartney would call him back and make it right. On the other hand, he really was fed up with it. But in the back of his mind, he was hoping Paul would have a "come to Jesus" moment.

"It was one of the hardest things I ever did in my life, to break off the relationship with a man I admired so much musically, what he had done in the world and in life, the best singer in the world, the best bass player, the best writer and crafter of songs; he was so meaningful in my life, so profound in my life. I just left that open to see what God had in store for me; what was next."

Seiwell had had a bond with this man, a friendship, and honestly could not understand how McCartney could overlook his struggles. There was such a disconnect. There was a friendship and yet Paul was causing a harsh reality of struggle in his life and didn't see it. It seemed so contrary and caused a lot of confusion and pain in Denny.

Ultimately, Seiwell did not hear from McCartney, and when he arrived home from a session on the night of September 28, Monique informed him that his father had passed away. They left for Pennsylvania the next morning to stay with Denny's mother for a little while. When they returned to London, they packed everything up and began to ship all their belongings to New York. Seiwell was getting calls for sessions in the U.K., but the pay was so small compared to the work in New York, where he made double and sometimes triple scale, that it didn't make sense.

As soon as the word got out that Seiwell was back in New York, the phone started ringing. The contractors were thrilled; nothing had really changed in that regard—but everything *felt* different. The allure was gone. After working with the greatest musician on the planet in a band like Wings, three sessions a day, oftentimes "polishing a turd," as they call it in the session world, was a huge let-down. It just felt like "going in, doing a job and getting paid."

At that point, Denny decided he needed to see a lawyer about suing McCartney for breach of promise. The attorney told him he had a case, but it might destroy his career.

At the end of 1973, Denny went back to London to play in Lou Reizner's four-night sold-out production of *Tommy* with the London Symphony Orchestra at the Rainbow Theatre. The orchestra was bolstered by a rock 'n' roll rhythm section featuring Seiwell on drums, Rick Wakeman on keyboards, and a bassist and guitarist from Australia. The cast included Roger Daltrey as Tommy, Keith Moon as Uncle Ernie, Peter Sellers, David Essex, and Merry Clayton as the Acid Queen.

"There was a 40-minute break in the show where there was no rock 'n' roll rhythm section—it was just all orchestra and singing—so Rick and I would run across the street to the pub and pound down a couple of drinks, then rush back just in time to sit down and play. The conductor was a guy by the name of David Measham, and it would piss him off. He'd say, 'You'd better not do that the night of the performance,' but we did. On the last night, they had a wrap party for us and Keith Moon and I started having fun together, and he invited me to his house Tara, and I spent the night."

Seiwell and Moon jumped into the limo to go out to Tara (Moon's home outside of London) and two girls jumped in after the drummers.

"I thought they were with him or that his wife had a girlfriend or something," Denny remembers. "But we left the party, and it was Keith and I and two girls. I knew one was with him, and I didn't know the other one, who was yacking like crazy. Keith looked at me and he was playing the rough mixes of *Quadrophenia.* I wanted to hear it and so did he, but we can't hear it because this girl is gabbing so much. He says, 'What's with this, mate?' I say, 'I don't even know who the fuck she is.' And he says, 'Don't worry about it.' We get to the house and he lays out three big lines of coke and a big line of Librium for her. This chick had 12 lines of Librium and she was still talking to herself the next day. We got up and she was still sitting in the living room, talking to herself, and Keith finally had his guy take her back and drop her in London."

Denny recalls that night listening to Moon's collection of music on his jukebox. "He hipped me to things like Tony Hancock, who was the British Lenny Bruce. It was a night I will never forget."

Around that same time in London, Seiwell was asked to play on Joe Cocker's *Put Out the Light* at the Who's studio in Battersea. Seiwell had known Cocker for a long time. He used to go by his place with McCullough in the early hours of the morning when the two were on a tear. When Denny was asked to play on some of the record, he was thrilled and said it was a great treat. "Nicky Hopkins was on keyboard, and there were some seriously great players on it." Unfortunately, they recorded it in the wrong key for Cocker, and when they re-recorded it, Seiwell was not available, so he ended up not being on the album.

Denny decided his next move should be a band. Henry McCullough was always, as he put it, his "mate." McCullough was preparing to record a solo

Denny reunites with old buddy Joe Cocker backstage at a Cocker show, Nokia Theater, Los Angeles, circa 2012. (Courtesy of Ray Neapolitan, Cocker's personal manager)

album, and Bill Oakes, a friend of Denny's who worked at Stigwood Records (RSO), set up a meeting for them with Robert Stigwood. McCullough and Seiwell presented Stigwood with the demo of McCullough's songs and a few days later Oakes confided that Stigwood, known to be gay, was hot on McCullough.

"When I told that to Henry, that freaked him out and he didn't want any part of it," Seiwell recalls. "But somehow or other, he cut some more demos and soon after that, we said, 'Why don't we do something together.'"

McCullough invited Chrissy Stewart, bassist from Spooky Tooth, and keyboardist/Hammond specialist Mick Weaver from Wynder K. Frog to form a band called Drueth. They approached Chris Blackwell at Island Records about the group, and told him they wanted to go to America.

Blackwell gave McCullough 5,000 pounds as start-up money and Stewart, Weaver and he flew over to Chicago to meet Denny and his friend Bill Young. Young had a company that made commercials; he and Denny had worked together many times with the artist Bill Quateman. Young said he was happy to help Denny start up this band. The band put some songs together and began cutting some demos and stayed maybe about a week. Seiwell's memories are a little cloudy on how word got to Elliot Mazer in San Francisco, but he brought them out there with the idea that he would find them work which they forged ahead on their own project. Young paid all their transport to San Francisco, equipment and all, and Mazer put them up in what Denny describes as a small turret castle which they treated like a flop house.

"We got in the studio and all of a sudden Elliot came up with all of these projects. Rab Noakes was one of the first ones, Mike D'Abo was the next one, there was a Juice Newton project, then Andy Fairweather Low."

In the mid-'70s, Denny worked a couple of weeks at the Boarding House with Mary Travers of Peter, Paul & Mary, which is when he bought cocaine from some musicians who invited him to a gig down in the city. He went to listen to them and told Mazer he would like to cut a demo with them; Mazer told him to go ahead. It was the band Pablo Cruise. Mazer, Gary Haber, the studio manager and Seiwell brought them to A&M who signed them, but Seiwell neglected to cut himself into the deal.

Mazer got a call from Janis Joplin's estate to re-cut some tracks on her final album. Denny says Joplin's vocals were amazing, but her band, Big Brother and the Holding Company, had to be replaced.

"We had the headphone balance with Janis in the middle and a little bit of Big Brother on the left side and a little bit more of our track on the right side," Seiwell recalls. "Janis was right on the money, but we had to kind of ignore Big Brother. We listened to it a couple of times, got the chords right and did the best we could. We recorded three, four, five songs that came out on the *Farewell Song* album."

The only one he can recall is "Misery'n," but he says the difference between the two bands is obvious.

"Our band Drueth was really good, and at the same time we were doing these projects, Elliot was getting us really good money because of our names and everything and in between projects, we were working on our repertoire and getting everything ready. Then Elliot set up a meeting with Ahmet Ertegun. Ahmet and his right-hand man Earl McGrath flew out to meet and hear the band, so we did a showcase for them in the studio. We didn't really have a lead singer, per se. Henry was our singer, and he wasn't an actual lead singer. He had good vocals, but we could have used someone who was a real front man. He left and then we heard from Elliot that he loved the band, but he had hung out with us all day and drank and did cocaine, so he said, 'I love these guys, but they scare the shit out of me,' and he bailed."

And yes, those were scary and dark days. Cocaine wasn't really Seiwell's addiction of choice, but he did dabble in it. The hangers-on liked being around high-profile musicians and were eager to supply them with perks. So Seiwell partook when it was available, even though he could take it or leave it. McCullough, on the other hand, indulged in all the extras the most.

"I'll never forget we stayed in a shitty motel in Shelter Bay between Sausalito and Mill Valley, with yellow formica countertops in the kitchen. They got some opium somewhere, and they would turn the gas stove on, heat up coat hangers and put the opium on the countertops. Then they would touch the opium with a coat hanger and take the coffee percolator stem and put it over it and suck the smoke up. I did it too, but I wasn't really into chasing the opium dragon. That was a little heavy for me. When we left that motel, that whole yellow countertop was black."

Meanwhile, Monique was in New York, hanging on to their roots and trying to get through the darkest moments of their marriage. She was working and living in a penthouse apartment she had found on 56th Street between 8th and 9th Avenues. It was one large room with a kitchen and bathroom with a big terrace.

"She felt we should be there, and I felt I had to parlay this McCartney thing into something that mattered. It was my opportunity to get a record deal and make hundreds of thousands of dollars. I had given three of my best earning years away and I had to turn it into some kind of financial reward. It was really screwed up."

THE FALLOUT

From the minute he moved to the West Coast, Denny's drinking increased. It didn't help that he was keeping the company of English and Irish blokes, but the whole McCartney episode had turned him into feeling like a loser. He had once been at the top of the heap as a New York first-call session guy who gave it up to be Paul McCartney's drummer, believing it was going to be magical—until the reality of 70 quid a week set in and the promise of being a shareholder in the band was never realized. While alcohol would numb the pain, it never impaired him so much that he couldn't show up or perform on a session to the best of his ability. Still, he considered himself a drunk.

"A drunk is when you can't stop drinking and you want to. That is someone like I was, who gets up and thinks about eliminating the pain I was in with alcohol, remembering all the sordid details of my life and getting screwed. Resentment. I would get really pissed off if someone asked, 'Hey what was it like playing with McCartney?' I blamed him for all my problems, and I couldn't wait to get to that stupid bar and hang out with my lowlife companions, who were in that same boat, so I felt a sense of family. They weren't really losers; they all had great careers, but for the most part, they were feeling somewhat like I was."

Denny says he drank as much as he could throughout the day. Sometimes he got up with a hangover, got a breakfast burrito and went to a bar for a beer with his burrito. By noon he began the heavier alcohol to deaden the feelings. "It was a horrible life."

Seiwell knew he was hitting bottom but couldn't stop it. He admits his state of mind was really messed up. For Denny, the stress of being the only American and having to rent the cars, find the apartments, put his name on the lease and take care of the banking because the other guys were not in the country legally contributed to the gallons of Scotch he was drinking. It was truly the lowest point of his life and his marriage. Denny was an emotional mess and with the two of them living on separate coasts, it felt as though they were growing apart at a very crucial moment in time.

"I would go to the grocery store and there would be two half gallons of Scotch and by the time we got it put away, they had finished one of them. Ahmet Ertigan was right. We were scary."

Monique and Denny were apart from February to July and then she joined him in Northern California. Amazingly, they survived the worst period of their marriage.

When Drueth eventually fizzled out and McCullough and Weaver moved down to the Santa Barbara area to join Joe Cocker's band, Denny was actually relieved. Stewart remained, and the two of them rented a house in Sausalito. Denny recalls when Chrissy's wife Pat flew in from Ireland, she met Chrissy and Monique in New York and Denny bought his 1971 rock 'n' roll Ford Thunderbird in Pennsylvania -- which Denny dubbed the Thunderchicken – to retrieve them. He picked them up in New York to drive back to California.

"The four-seater was loaded; we drove across the country with two people in the front, two people in the backseat—Chrissy and Pat with a cat in between—a bunch of bags and a television. What a nightmare that was, but we were young," Denny recalls with a laugh.

After they returned to California, Seiwell and Stewart continued to do sessions with such people like Juice Newton, Andy Fairweather Low and one with Keith and Donna Godchaux of Grateful Dead fame. They called Denny to share the recording of their solo album, *Keith & Donna,* with Bernard Purdie. "The whole album was laid back. It was cocaine, Maalox and Heineken. Come to think of it, I don't remember ever hearing the record, but I think it was pretty good," Denny says with a laugh. "I got to meet Jerry Garcia, and I did a live gig in '75 at the Great American Music Hall with him and Merl Saunders, which was really a trip, but I don't remember much about it because I was pretty messed up back then."

He recalls another funny story when he invited Van Morrison over to meet Stewart and his wife Pat. Morrison lived just north of Sausalito and Denny had done some work with him in his home studio. Hailing from Ireland as well, Stewart and his wife, Pat, were huge fans of Morrison's, so Denny asked Morrison if he'd want to come over and meet his Irish bass player and his wife. Morrison said sure.

"Van used to go sober and then not sober. He'd give it up for a little while and then he'd go back at it. This was one of those times when he had given it up, so he came over and he was super quiet and super weird. Chrissy and Pat didn't know what to do. When he left it was, 'Thank God he's gone.'"

Also, in 1975 Stewart and Seiwell started getting calls to travel to Los Angeles for work occasionally. On one trip, they met with Michael Des Barres and Michael Monarch, who played guitar with Steppenwolf. They formed a band called Buck, and Seiwell says they had a bunch of really great songs.

"(Monarch) was like a modern-day Keith Richards, and we decided to put a band together. De Barres was our frontman and lead singer. We were managed by Sepp Donahower, who ran Pacific Presentations, one of the biggest promoters in town. Sepp was kinda backing us and putting money into us. He set up a million-dollar record deal with CBS Records and we did a couple of gigs; Sepp and both Michaels came up from L.A. to San Francisco and we did a TV show called *The Mallory Earl Show*."

One night, on the way to a gig outside of San Francisco, they dodged a bullet. Seiwell thinks that Monique was driving, but maybe a little too fast, and the car was loaded with drugs.

"We were in that old Thunderchicken and we got pulled over on one of those bridges. I thought, 'That's it, we're going to jail!' Chrissy didn't have a green card or anything, but for some reason or another, (the cop) just let us go. He didn't search us or anything. If he had, he would have hit paydirt!"

Later on, they weren't so lucky. "At one point, CBS gave Sepp Donahower $50,000 sight unseen and they wanted first shot at the deal for that million-dollar record deal. We were all at the Rainbow one night waiting for Sepp to finish his meeting and to give us some money. We didn't just sit at a bar; we drank," Seiwell recalls. "We were doing what rock 'n' roll bands did back then: sitting in a booth, drinking, talking about how great it was going to be when we got this record deal, and Sepp came in and said, 'I don't know how to tell you this, but they passed on the deal.' The deal fell through, and we had a bar tab that was over $100. Sepp didn't even pay the tab. We were staying at the Beverly Rodeo, which was a little boutique hotel on Rodeo Drive and I'm driving a rental car down Doheny and I'm pissed off and I'm driving too fast, and a cop pulls us over. We went to jail that night. They took Michael Monarch, my roadie and me and locked the three of us up."

They put Monarch in a separate cell because he was dressed in a black tux with a frilly ladies' blouse, ballet slippers and he had a small bag with a rubber nose air horn inside. He was high on angel dust. In the morning, they brought them all pancakes, and Denny laughs as he recalls asking the guard for cream for his coffee.

Denny called Gary Haber in San Francisco, who he believes called Donahower, and they worked together in getting the three of them out of jail. Stewart and Denny drove back to San Francisco the following day.

AN AWKWARD ICE-BREAKING

In 1975, while touring with Stephen Stills and his first wife Veronique Sanson, Denny saw McCartney for the first time since he left Wings. Denny didn't know Stills previously, but the connection was made through the San Francisco studio His Master's Wheels, and Seiwell was happy to take the gig. Ahead of four nights at the Paris Olympia Theatre, they rehearsed outside Paris in a mansion that had been used in World War II by the Gestapo, Seiwell recounts. Joe Lala was in the band, as well as some of Sanson's band members and Denny says Veronique Sanson was—and still is—amazing. After Paris, Stills suggested they go to London to see Paul and Linda, and asked Denny to give them a call to see if they were around.

"This was about a year and a half after I left the band and I hadn't spoken to them at all," Seiwell says. "I said, 'Well, ok. I called London and I said, 'Hey Paul, how ya doin'?' He said, 'Oh Denny, how are you?' It was a welcoming phone call. I said, 'I'm here in Paris with Stills. We just did four nights with his wife, and we'd like to come up and see you and have dinner with you.'

And he said, 'Sure, that'd be great, come on up. We'd love to see you and Stephen.' I thought, 'What the hell?' I thought he was still mad at me for leaving the way I left. I said, 'Monique's here,' and he said, 'Great, bring her along.'"

Stills rented a private plane for the 45-minute trip from Paris to London. There was a green fastback Bentley waiting for them that Stills had just purchased, and they proceeded to the McCartney home.

"We had dinner with them, and it was lovely, but I was so nervous about seeing them again and didn't know what to make of it, so I was kind of a mess. But they were happy to see us."

PLANTING ROOTS IN LOS ANGELES

His Master's Wheels, Elliot Mazer's studio in San Francisco where Denny did a lot of projects post-Wings. (Courtesy of Elliot Mazer)

Shortly thereafter, Stewart ended up moving back to England and the Seiwells moved down to Los Angeles into the Oakwood Apartments, which were temporary apartments where people could get their bearings while looking for permanent residence. Denny tried to spread word that he was available for work, and he signed up for the popular answering service of the time, Your Girl.

Seiwell's business manager Gary Haber moved to Los Angeles as well, opening offices for Rosen, Cohen, Erlich and Haber and helped to line up some work for Denny, but the music scene didn't know quite what to make of him. Many thought he was an English rock 'n' roller, not remembering that he was an American jazz musician first, or a session drummer in New York. Denny would do his best to network; Haber was an integral assistant. He took him to a party at the Rolling Stone's manager's home in Benedict Canyon, where Seiwell recalls seeing Larry Hagman in a gorilla suit and a "bunch of crazy shit."

"We'd get so drunk, and we'd drive back home over the canyon," Denny remembers. "I'd have to get up and wash my car the next day. I remember one day going down to Hollywood and having a meeting at the apartment of the manager of the Chili Peppers, who were just getting started, and a woman kept pounding on the floor because we were making too much noise."

His bassist friend Chuck Domanico also helped get Denny on the radar of writers and musicians in Los Angeles. One project, among others, that Seiwell recalls Domanico got him, was with piano player Lincoln Mayorga, who was recording Margie Gibson. "If he hadn't spread the word that I was in town, I just would have gotten drunk every day. I was really having a tough time of it."

There were a few Richard Perry sessions during that period including two cuts of Art Garfunkel's 1975 *Breakaway,* one of which is the very popular "99 Miles from L.A." Garfunkel is known for being difficult. But Perry could be difficult too. Brooks Arthur was the engineer and a buddy of Denny's from his New York days.

Seiwell recalls a session at Perry's then-newly opened Studio 55 for a Pointer Sisters project. After the first take Perry said to him, "Denny, that was perfect, don't change a thing," and proceeded to move his entire set around—his hi-hat to the left, the cymbal back a little. "He was having trouble recording it, getting it on tape." By the end of the session, he had changed everything.

Later in the year, he did two back-to-back Manhattan Transfer sessions in one day with Perry. Denny wishes he can remember the night he got the call to play the China Club on Selma in Hollywood on a Monday and was told he was on stage at one point with Joe Walsh, Elton John and John Entwhistle. In March of '75, Seiwell was called to play at the Record Plant's Jim Keltner Fan Club Jam Session one Sunday night when Jim could not make it. He played with Mick Jagger and assorted members of hot bands at the time. "I'll never forget that Mick wanted to do a samba," Denny says.

On March 15,1975 Denny got a call about the Wings settlement. Denny was to meet with a representative from McCartney's management by the name of Brian Brolley at the Beverly Wilshire Hotel. Brolley told Seiwell that McCartney was trying to finally make the situation right, but he offered him a totally unacceptable amount. As Seiwell's memory serves, Brolley was asking him to sign off on all future claims to Wings' earnings in return for the payment, telling Denny, "We don't even have to give you this." Seiwell wanted to tear up the check; it was a totally absurd amount for his contribution to Wings. But money was very tight for the Seiwells, and Denny finally said he'd be happy to take the check—but absolutely would not agree to those terms. It would be another 26 years before Seiwell received a real settlement for his contribution to the band he helped start.

Denny and Monique visiting backstage 1976 in Chicago during Wings Over America tour. (All rights reserved.)

In April, Denny recorded with Don Preston again in San Francisco at His Master's Wheels, and by May 1st the Seiwells had moved to L.A.

Starting in mid-1975, Denny was flying back and forth to Chicago to co-produce (with John Stronach) and play on a record for Bill Quateman. After commuting from L.A. for nearly a year, in April, 1976 the Seiwells moved into a large studio apartment with floor-to-ceiling windows overlooking the lake in Chicago. The project was supposed to take three months, but there were financial problems funding the project, so it took much longer. Seiwell says that Quateman was a good artist, signed by Arista Records and Clive Davis. Percussionist Lenny Castro was in the band. They did some live dates to make some money, and Denny did some jingle work for his friend Bill Young. At the end of September, Denny and Stronach traveled to L.A. to mix the album at the Record Plant.

Sometime in 1977, Seiwell began to worry about his drinking, and decided to see a doctor. He saw Dr. Ralph Gold, to whom a lot of musicians went, since he was a musician himself. Because of this, musicians felt they could tell Dr. Gold the truth about their vices. Denny told him, "I think I have a problem with alcohol." And the good doctor replied, "Well, if you have a problem with alcohol, there's only one thing that works: a 12-step program." Not quite ready to accept that solution, Denny said, "What else you got?"

At a certain point, although Seiwell can't recall the timeline, he tried hypnosis and says it helped for a brief period. He also says that when he was working, he didn't feel the need to drink quite as much, because he felt valued. But when he wasn't working or between jobs, that's when he was at his worst.

RICK DANKO AND LEON RUSSELL

In 1977, Seiwell played with the Rick Danko Band, which he says was like being in The Band. He comments that the Danko Brothers—Terry and Rick—had sensational vocals together. The band consisted of the Dankos, Seiwell, Walt Richmond (piano), Michael DeTemple (guitar), Jerry Peterson (saxophone), and Marty Grebb (organ, guitar and saxophone). Denny says the band called Rick Danko "Bingo Beyondo," "because he was so loveable, a sweetheart of all times, always out of his mind and full of energy even though he did a lot of drugs. He was always there."

"We did a couple of TV shows: *In Concert, Midnight Special.* We toured the States and Japan," Denny recounts, adding that playing double drums live with Gregg Thomas was lots of fun. "We had the distinction of doing that whole tour without getting undressed and going to bed at night. We fell asleep fully dressed on top of the bed. I remember one night in Japan we were particularly gone, and we had the Japanese press come up to a suite they had put us in for this press conference. This suite had these very treasured Japanese dolls in glass cases; you don't mess around with them. The press was there with all their cameras and microphones, and Rick went over and opened up one of those glass cases and pulled a doll out and lifted up the skirt and pretended he was giving it head. We were nuts!"

Later on, Danko had the Rick Danko Revival Show with Gary Busey and Paul Butterfield. Busey had just finished *The Buddy Holly Story* film so he would do about six of those songs with the band. "Butter, Busy and Danko, it was madness," Seiwell says. "The whole band was like that, but when we turned up to play, it was magic."

They played five nights at the Roxy in L.A. A&M's Jerry Moss rented them two mobile home trailers parked next to the venue because there was no way the venue could accommodate the amount of people upstairs in the VIP area.

"I remember sitting in there one night. We had said, 'Guys, don't bring any guests in here; this is for the band only.' Everybody was there. Each night was good, and each night was incredibly insane. Jerry Moss tried to come into our mobile home, and I said, 'Band only. Piss off, whoever you are.' Then they told me, 'That's Jerry Moss; that's the guy who's paying for this thing!' I knew who Herb Alpert was, but not Jerry Moss. I had no idea."

They recorded in a Malibu studio called Shangri La with Rob Fraboni producing. Seiwell started to do some projects with Fraboni, like Jennifer Warnes' *Shot Through the Heart* (1979) at Village Studios. Seiwell says the record, which also featured Andrew Gold and Abraham Laboriel, Sr., was one of the better records he did. It spawned four semi-hit singles.

Fraboni called him for a Neil Young session, which Seiwell says was the strangest date he has ever done. They went into the small room at Village Studios. Denny doesn't recall the other players, but thinks Abe Labroriel, Sr. may have been the bass player.

"Neil came in and said, 'I don't have any music for you to play, but what I want you guys to do is, I'm going to talk about a dream I had, and I want you guys to play anything that comes to mind,'" Denny recalls. "We just all looked at each other like, 'What is this? And how much are we getting paid? Not only are we playing, but we are composing whatever this is and it's going to be really weird.' So he starts talking about this dream about how something comes falling out of the sky and lands on a baby in a baby carriage and squashed it. I didn't know if I should do a rimshot or what! It was just one of those experimental moments. I'm sure it was never used, but we just jammed and got a little groove going. We'd hear something while he talked about the dream and just took it into another direction. We all looked at each other and laughed. It was probably on my list of the top three weirdest things that ever happened."

One of the other bizarre dates Denny remembers was for a 1977 Liza Minnelli record, *Tropical Nights*, engineered by Rik Pekkonen, noting the cut which is a medley of the title track and *Bali Ha'i* a la disco.

"It was 13 pages of music," Seiwell recalls. "I had it strung up between the two overhead mics. I had it stretched to the left and I would read across to the right and by the time I would get all the way to the last page, I had a stiff neck. Thank God I could see well at that point; I didn't have glasses yet. She came out at one point and said, 'Guys, guys, it doesn't go like that, it goes like this…' and she started dancing. That's another weird one: 'It goes like this…' and she started dancing!"

That memory reminds Seiwell of one night in 1969 (June 15) when he saw Judy Garland right before she died (June 22). He was in the house band at the Half Note in New York City, playing with Al Cohn, Zoot Sims and Anita O'Day. Garland was on her way to London and stopped in to see her old friend Anita O'Day; Judy was very drunk, as she often was in those last days.

"They got her up on stage and Dave Frishberg was playing piano and she sang 'Over the Rainbow,' 'April Showers' and one more of her big hits, and as messed up as she was, it was magical. Apparently, it was the last night she ever performed."

In 1978 Rob Stoner, Bob Dylan's musical director, asked Denny to do a world tour with the icon. He didn't really want to leave his studio career, but Stoner convinced him to go down and check out the band, which he did, and he did like the band a lot. They made him an offer he couldn't refuse, and the next day he brought his passport and all the paperwork down to the business people for the visa for the world tour.

"They came back and told Bob they couldn't take me along on the tour because I had been busted with Paul McCartney in Sweden back in 1972, therefore I wouldn't be able to go into Japan or Australia, which wasn't correct information. But it got me out of the tour, which I really didn't want to do, although playing with Dylan really would have been wonderful. But I didn't want to go out of town for a long period of time."

Happily, it worked out that way because one of his dream jobs occurred right about then, with Leon Russell.

Russell had seen that Denny had just been working with Rick and Terry Danko, and asked him to work with him. Seiwell was thrilled. But he remembers how odd it was when Russell told him, "I never thought I could get you to work with me if you were Paul McCartney's drummer," because Denny always thought coming from McCartney it would be easy to break into the scene, but instead it was kind of working against him. It was keeping people from actually approaching him.

Seiwell absolutely loved Russell; he was a huge fan. "He put me on retainer. Marty Grebb and I would go over to his house every day, pretty much Monday through Friday, and record. He had a house in Toluca Lake with a house in the back with a studio in it, and it had a 40-track Stephens in it, which, at the time, was unheard of. Roger Linn was in the band, too. Then one day he said to come over to his film studio, which was right across from Evergreen Recording Studios in North Hollywood. It was the first time I played live with Leon. Leon had that Yamaha electric baby grand piano, and we were in there running down some tunes. Maybe he was planning on taking us on the

Trouble in Tokyo: Rick Danko tour, 1976. L-R: Jerry Peterson, Denny, Terry Danko, Juni (Arista records rep). (Courtesy of Marty Grebb)

road, I don't know. And he was filming everything. We were playing along on one of the tunes, and I was right behind Leon up on the riser. He'd look over to me and motion, 'go to the ride here,' or 'go to the hi-hat here.' That was just the way he heard it. If anyone else had done that to me, I would have thrown a stick at them—I didn't like it when people told me how to play the drums—but it wasn't nasty the way he did it. And I'll be damned if he wasn't right."

In 1979 Seiwell recorded Russell's single "Anita Bryant" and the record *Heart of Fire* with Mary Russell (to whom Leon was married at the time). "Leon was really special," Denny comments.

In October 1979, Red Young, the musical director for Joan Armatrading, contacted Denny to join her band for an Australian tour, when Richie Hayward couldn't perform due to a motorcycle accident. There was no time to rehearse a drummer, so they needed someone who could read. Denny had been working with Young in a few configurations, including the Shelby Flint Band, so he recommended him. Seiwell went to Young's house, and they had a couple of rehearsals to run through the show. Seiwell says the music was quite demanding.

"There was one song where the chart was scribbled all over, and I made all sorts of notes on it. I thought, 'If I have to read this chart like this, it could be bad.' I had some music paper with me and I recopied the part, so I could have it be precise. Unfortunately, the only pen I had with me was a green pen and when I put it on the stand to do the show and the lights hit it, it all disappeared. But by copying it, I remembered most of it, and I kinda got through it."

The travel was demanding as well. The flight to Australia was tough. He had worked all day in the studio and was on a 10:30 p.m. flight that was to last about 24 hours.

"On the way to the airport, I smoked about a half dozen joints. I thought I'd get real high and sleep. I told the stewardess, 'Just keep pouring scotch down me until I pass out.'"

Armatrading had to attend to medical issues during the tour, so the band had to return home and then go back to Australia for the re-booked dates. The two trips to Australia were exhausting, but Seiwell says the music was great, and so was Armatrading.

When he returned to L.A., Denny returned to recording. Other albums around that time included Danny Peck, Mark Wirtz with Richard Bennett, and one with Sneaky Pete. The work began to dwindle due to sampling and computers, and Denny began to get more into orchestral and film work. "My regular jingle account was aware of my growing addiction, so I'd leave the studio and eight minutes later I'd walk into my bar. They'd call and say, 'Is Denny there?' And they'd say, 'He just walked in.' 'Send him back, I'm not done with him.'" Seiwell says those residuals kept him alive. "Those days were special because they were before the drum machine came along and screwed it all up."

When the work was flowing, Denny was happy. He enjoyed standing in line at the union to pick up his checks.

"We'd stand in line with pride if we had money there," Seiwell recalls. "And then I'd go across the street to Pro Drum Shop and Bob Yeager would say some wise-ass remark like, 'Oh, you again,' which meant that you were accepted and 'in.' When Bob messed with you a little, it meant you were one of the cats."

Between the studio sessions, Denny formed another band with guitarist Don Preston called Driving Wheel that he describes as Southern blues rock, and he worked on another project called *Gone* with Jerry Williams. Williams (nicknamed "scary") was a guitarist and piano player who had a serious drug problem. He was a prolific songwriter who wrote a lot of songs for Eric Clapton, among others. Seiwell played half the tracks on *Gone*, and Jeff Porcaro played most of the others. Seiwell notes one particular cut, "I've Got Dreams to Remember," with guitarist Steve Cropper and bassist Duck Dunn. "It just makes you cry, it's so beautiful. (Williams) was probably one of the most talented guys I have ever come across," Denny recalls. "He was like a White, Texas, redneck, biker guy that sounded like Stevie Wonder."

The mention of Jeff Porcaro conjures up another story – a double-drum session with Jeff on Friday, June 13, 1975. During the time he was playing in Buck, Denny ran into Steve Marriott one night at the famed Rainbow on Sunset Blvd.

"When I got drunk, I was a social butterfly. I ended up sitting and talking to Steve Marriott. He said, 'Ya know, I'm going into the studio tomorrow, A&M, and I'd like you to come play on this track with me.' I said, 'Awww, come on, that's the cocaine talking.' He said, 'I'm serious, call your cartage company and get your drums delivered.' I said, 'Come on man, just forget it.' He said 'I'm dead serious. Please call your cartage company. I'm booking you for the session right now. Are you available?' I said, 'Yes, but you have to have a drummer booked already,' and he said, 'I do, but I'd like to have double drums—you and Jeff Porcaro.' I said, 'You don't need me if you have Jeff Porcaro!' But he talked me into it. I had my drums delivered, but it was last-minute, and my cartage company didn't bring a complete set. I was missing pieces. Jeff had all his gear, plus some leftover gear, so he could make it happen for me. We recorded. I don't recall if it was one or two tracks that day, but it was brilliant. I loved it, he loved it," Denny recalls. There was a keen telepathy between the two drummers: "We would just look at each other and either he would lead into something or create a vibe or I would. We didn't talk about it; it was all unsaid. We just played as one, but influenced by each of our ideas of what was musical and spontaneous. He loved double drums."

Denny knew Jeff since Porcaro was a teenager. Jeff's father Joe would bring him into Donte's back in 1968 to see Denny play with Roger Kellaway, Tom Scott and Chuck Domanico when he'd be in Los Angeles. "Sometimes Joe would bring all three of the boys," Seiwell recalls.

To his knowledge, that Marriott record was never released. "That's one of the treasures in my life I could never find," says Denny. (On a side note, he terminated his cartage company that day.)

On June 30, 1975, Denny was called in to audition for Linda Ronstadt, but he didn't get the job. He recalls another time getting hired to play for a 10-week tour with Bette Midler. They were rehearsing at S.I.R. and Seiwell thinks he may have said something chauvinistic in jest.

"I came home from rehearsal that day and Aaron Russo, her manager, called me and said, 'Go back and get your drums, we got another guy. Your services won't be needed.'"

Midler's regular drummer had actually become available, but Denny had put 10 weeks on hold, so it became the only time he went to the union to file a claim, which took six months, but he was compensated. (In cases like this, the musician's union is there to protect a member musician when contracts are broken and musicians do not get paid. The union files a suit against the employer who hired the musician.)

Seiwell mentions *Framed*, a notable record he did in 1979 with Dave Lambert of the Strawbs (guitar/vocals), featuring John Entwistle, Richard Bennett, Tom Hensley and Lee Sklar. He believes it was the first time he worked with Sklar. "The record was very classy, with the greatest people in town on it. The music was great."

TELEVISION

In the '80s Seiwell had begun getting calls for television work on shows like

Happy Days, Laverne and Shirley, Knots Landing (12/79-5/93), *The Practice* (3/97-5/2004), *Flamingo Road* (1981-1982) and *Thirty Something* (9/87-5/93). Some of the earlier ones were probably calls for what is called library music, which Denny describes as a session where musicians would record a bunch of cues of varying lengths that the production would use at their discretion on different episodes, as opposed to some of the other shows on which he was scheduled on a weekly basis. One such weekly show—his favorite—was *Homefront*, which ran from 1991-1993.

"It was about the guys coming back from World War II, so it included big band music from that time period. I just loved it because growing up my dad played with the big bands and I had a fondness for that type of music," Denny says. " I was the youngest guy in the band, with guys like Chauncey Welsch (trombone), Lloyd Elliott (trombone), Ronnie Lang (alto sax), Gene Cipriano (woodwinds); all these guys who played with Benny Goodman and Woody Herman. Stewart Levin wrote the music for it." One day, Levin was so enamored of a cue that Denny played that before Denny had even gotten home, Levin had mixed it and sent it to him, telling him how incredible he thought it was. "The show was so great. Every week I would have a four-hour session booked and there would be two or three hours of jokes and an hour's worth of recording. With these guys it was like going to a high school reunion; everybody was so glad to be seeing each other on the same date. Warren Luening (trumpet), Rick Baptist (trumpet)—incredible musicians, every one of them. It was so much fun. It was heartbreaking when it was over," Seiwell says, adding that the television work gave him credibility and let it be known that he was not an English rock 'n' roll drummer like many thought, but a skilled reader who could play it all.

Drummer Ralph Humphrey (Frank Zappa, Natalie Cole, Wayne Shorter, etc.) called Denny one day to sub on an animated TV show called *Animaniacs* (1993-1998), which Humphrey regularly recorded on the Paramount lot. Humphrey said there would be a small 40-piece orchestra and he told him that his equipment would be there. All Denny had to do was show up and play. Seiwell knew cartoon music was difficult, but he accepted the challenge.

"I went down there, and in his area there was a lot of equipment—bells, vibraphone—and the music had to be situated right so you could lean over and hit a couple of bells or whatever. I was having a ball, but there was this one cue, and I screwed it up three times in a row, which was unheard of for me. They had to take a break. They have to get so many minutes worth of music in during each session, so they had to go back to it at the end of the session and had to have me re-record it I guess, but I said to myself, 'This is it, I'll never work for these people again.' I felt terrible, so on the ten-minute break I took the score into the control room to the music copyist and I said, 'Can we do a bar count here? I just want to see what's going on.' So I said, 'Ok, here's 35, 36, 37. 37 is a 3/4 bar, right?' And she said, 'No, no, 37 is a 4/4 bar,' and I went, 'Oh my God!' I was reading it correctly, but there was a mistake on the part. I went up to the composers and said, 'I'm really sorry about this. I know I'm just filling in for Ralph who does this in his sleep, but I just checked with the music copyist and there's a mistake on my part. It says bar 37 is a 3/4 bar, but it's (actually) a 4/4 bar. No wonder we didn't come out together.' And he said, 'Yeah, you're right, man. I'm glad you told me that, because we'd never call you again.' And guess what? He never called me again anyway! I read the music, that's all I can do. But I'm glad I had the wherewithal to go talk to the copyist and go over the bar count to find out what the problem was, because I don't screw up like that," Seiwell says, adding that he and Humphrey had a good laugh about the whole incident.

FILM WORK

Denny began getting film work calls in the mid-'90s. Although he had done the main title track for *Harper Valley PTA* (at Universal) and *Grease 2* in 1981 (which was treated as more of a record date, with only a rhythm section at Evergreen Studios), these were much earlier, and he can't recall exactly how the legit film calls began. They may have generated from his buddy Chuck Domanico, who put in a good word with contractor Sandy DeCrescent (with whom he had already done some of the television work). Another possibility is the rekindling of his friendship with James Newton Howard from way back in the mid-'70s, when James was playing with Melissa Manchester and both he and Seiwell were living at the Oakwood Apartments. James Newton Howard began to call Denny to play on a lot of his film projects, such as *Waterworld* (1995), *Postman* (1997), *A Perfect Murder* (1998), *Dinosaurs* (2000), *Vertical*

Recording James Newton Howard's score for *Waterworld*, Todd-AO Studios, L.A., 1995. (Photo by Emil Richards)

Limit (2000), *Atlantis: The Lost Empire* (2001). Seiwell believes the protocol was that Howard had to request him on the project in the beginning because, DeCrescent had her list of regulars that she would call. The scores for 1997's *Metro* and 1998's *Murder of Crows*, on which Denny played drums, were written by Steve Porcaro.

According to Denny, in these major orchestral film recordings sessions, there is "usually a 110-piece symphony orchestra with a six-, seven- or eight-piece percussion section. It was always Joe Porcaro, Larry Bunker, Emil Richards, Bob Zimmitti, Mike Fisher, Peter Limonick on timpani; some of the finest players in the world. I was very fortunate to get a chance to work with these guys and really shed my classical chops together and play the legit style of drumming. Most of the time I wasn't even playing drums, although I did play some piccolo snare and marching field drum. Usually my task would be the bass drum to keep the orchestra swinging. I had to be an intense reader. It was a lot of fun; something most rock 'n' roll drummers don't get a chance to do."

The first time Howard asked Denny if he'd like to work on one of the films, Denny said yes. He was excited about the prospect but naturally had some trepidation. With the date looming the following week, he called his old friend Joe Porcaro.

"I knew Joe was going to be the percussion leader, so I said, 'Joe, can I come up to the house and spend some time with you?' Joe knew my playing, but he didn't know my reading capability. So, he gave me one of the sight-reading tests from Musicians Institute that was incredibly difficult, and I flunked it with flying colors. But he knew I could read, just by the way I handled it, and that my reading was good because I had done other things with him; he had seen me work on TV shows and things. But now I was graduating to this other world of orchestra dates which requires classical musicians, not a jazz guy or a rock guy."

Playing with an orchestra wasn't brand new for Denny. After all, "Live and Let Die" was with a 40-piece orchestra, and even before that, in New York he had recorded with orchestras, and in the Navy sometimes as well. But what he was about to embark on was about as high caliber as it would get.

Seiwell says there wasn't really anything he could do to prepare for the reading. He knew the test Joe had given him was way beyond anything he would ever encounter on a film score, and he also knew that both Joe and James were

Rounding up 110 musicians after a 10-minute break can sometimes be difficult. (Photo by Denny Seiwell)

confident that he could handle it. When Denny arrived at the *Waterworld* date at the massive Todd-AO soundstage the following week, there were seven percussionists. James put him on the bass drum (gran casa) "because you have great time and there is going to be a lot of music and a lot of chase scenes and the orchestra needs good time on the bass drum."

"Even though you are working with a click track, the bass drum has to be right on top of the click so they keep the orchestra up in tempo, so it fits the film frame by frame," explains Denny. "The bass drum is very crucial. I remember one day the strings were lagging so much one day that Larry Bunker, in his inimitable way, said, 'Strings, click, click.' He put the fear of death in them. Larry was one of the most musical musicians ever. So, I was on the bass drum, and I was looking at the music and it was complicated with a lot of odd times: 1,2,3, 1,2, 1,2,3, 1,2, 1,2,3, 1,2—that's playing in 5/8 time. You can make a mistake once. You can even make a second mistake, but if you make a third mistake, you're done; that part of your career is over—go back to playing rock 'n' roll. So I was on edge. My friend Chuck Domanico was in the bass section, so I'd go over and hide out with him on the breaks. The guys accepted me, but you could tell I was on a trial run. It really meant a lot to me to be able to do this. I pulled out all my experience and training to do a good job. If anything, I wouldn't know quite how hard to hit the bass drum, because it was a huge bass drum that you would dampen with your knee."

The process itself was something Seiwell had to learn. They used a little transistor radio which he wore on his belt.

"We weren't wearing big headphones. I had one earphone in my ear and the orchestra tempo was coming in the ear through the little radio, so you could run from one side of the stage to another to hit another instrument. I had to go buy the radio and find out how to use it, set it up at a certain station, and in the booth, they would broadcast the click. They'd give you like four warning clicks, and the orchestra would begin to play. You'd have to turn off and turn on the radio every hour or so, or it would stop working. One time we were in the big, long, hard-ass chase scene odd-time cue and the fuckin' radio went out on me. I had to stay with it and feel it until the take stopped and I didn't blow it."

Seiwell cut his teeth on *Waterworld,* which he recalls took about 5-7 days. He loved every minute of the film work. Sessions went from 10:00 a.m. to 6:00 p.m., and by the time he would hit the house, he definitely needed a nap, feeling depleted, yet fulfilled.

Denny called Monique on a break late in the week of the Waterworld sessions and asked if she could leave work a little early to come by the studio. "I said, 'Come to Radford Street and just drive onto the CBS lot like you're supposed to be there. Park the car and come into the building like you own it. Come right into the studio—unless the red light is on, because there is a 110-piece orchestra.' She parked, walked in and didn't see a red light, but she could slightly hear that there was some music, so she opened the door and walked in. I was in the very back of the room right in the center with the bass drum. I could see her right in my line of vision and the orchestra was in the middle of one of those emotional string cues. I could see that Monique was swept away, hearing the orchestra live. It was unbelievable. I could see tears starting to well up and I started to well up, too, standing there in the back. The guys were looking at me like, 'What the hell is going on?' It was a very special moment and a memory I will never forget."

On the sessions, the Straw Boss would hand out the parts. Then the musicians would take a colored marker and highlight their parts so they could see them coming up and play them on time.

Denny says he doesn't recall the film, but the most challenging musical moment that occurred in his career was an important cue that required two piccolo snare drums. Joe Porcaro and he were to play them on opposite sides of the stage, quite a distance apart, and they had to be played in unison, so they sounded like one drum.

"They had to be measured rolls, which would be 15 strokes, played like one drum," Denny remembers. "I probably peed my pants. I woodshedded it on the break, measured the rolls out, and made sure I knew how to play it. It was in triple pianissimo too, so it was as light as it could possibly be played—at a whisper. We had a few run-throughs because the orchestra needed it too, and we did a couple of takes and pulled it off."

Seiwell recalls that Emil Richards was so good that he could catnap between cues. "He would sit at his mallets and the music would be going crazy and he would be asleep. He would wake up and pick up a set of mallets and play the most ridiculously hard part and go back to sleep."

The animated films like *Dinosaurs* and *Atlantis* were especially difficult for Denny because there was a lot of music in them.

Film work was a great paying job—residual income and all—but in addition to that, it was a tremendously musically rewarding experience. "Not many people who get to play with someone like Paul McCartney get to play in that kind of setting," Seiwell says.

Seiwell recalls those days with fondness. If he wasn't working on a film, he was on a TV session or a record date. If he wasn't booked on any of those, he would have time to take a demo session. "Writers would call you to lay down a track for a demo and they were always fun because it was light."

To this day, Seiwell is not certain why his film calls stopped. He theorizes that it was political between contractors, but he'll never know for sure. And then the guard changed.

THE AFM STRIKE AND THE DRUM MACHINE

In August 1980 the American Federation of Musicians took to the picket lines to strike against the Association of Motion Picture and Television Producers. What that meant was musicians could not record for television or film. At that time, Seiwell was recording four or five television shows every season through the contractors of the day, like Jules Chakin, Sandy DeCrescent and Carl Fortina, to whom Chuck Domanico had made initial introductions. The strike was devastating for the workaday musicians, as it lasted 167 days.

To add insult to injury, around the same time as the strike, in 1980, Roger Linn released his first incarnation of the Linn Drum Machine, the LM-1. Just the year before, Denny and Linn had been in Leon Russell's band together. He had no idea what Linn was up to. It came as a complete shock when the machine was unveiled.

"I always said if I had known he was developing the Linn machine, I would have stumbled over it and delayed the progress of it by at least a few months or a couple of years. 'Oops, sorry Roger,'" he says with a laugh. "People thought they could get what they needed without having to give a drummer a break every hour. For a while I tried to go along with it. I got live cymbals and Remo practice pads with triggers in them and made my own kind of set-up, because the Simmons drums were just not doing it. I had the 14th set of Simmons drums in Los Angeles. I would get calls for sessions for that Simmons sound or you could rent them out to the composer or the session. But they were horrible to play on; they were like a tabletop surface."

A mishap occurred with his drum tech and the delivery of his Simmons drums for a Lalo Schifrin session one day, contracted by Carl Fortina, who called Denny for a lot of work. There are two Paramount locations: the recording studio on Santa Monica and the lot on Melrose. His drum tech delivered the Simmons drums to the recording studio and not the lot where he was supposed to take them.

"I had never worked with Lalo Schifrin before and he was one of the greats, so I was very excited. I walked in and I said, 'Uh oh! They're not here?' And he said, 'No.' I called my tech. Carl had a date booked there too, but he went to the wrong Paramount. I told him to get them over ASAP. They had to start the session with a ten-minute break, which they don't like to do. My tech picked up the drums and drove on the sidewalk to get them over there. We finally did the take, but I never heard from Lalo Schifrin again. It was a legitimate mistake. That shit happens."

Television work was a great source of income and provided residual checks. And Seiwell says it connected him with great people like percussionist Victor Feldman on a show at Universal Studios.

"I don't remember what show it was, but I loved Victor. He wrote the song 'Seven Steps to Heaven' for Miles Davis. On one cue, he ran to the marimbas and played the most incredible, burning marimba part and then just laid down the mallets like it was nothing. I just couldn't believe it because really, he was a piano player; he was on the session as a piano player. That's where Victor and I really bonded, and he invited me to join a trio with Chuck Domanico on bass. We would rehearse out at his house; he had a studio in the back, and we would play at Le Cafe. We had a gig there and rehearsed a set of music that was Chopin for a jazz trio. It was tremendous. This gig was with John Patitucci, who was just breaking into the scene, and he was phenomenal. Victor's wife Marilyn, who passed away shortly after that, had a little cassette player, was there that night and recorded the set and I still have that. It was brilliant. I probably have the only copy today; I burned it onto a CD and it's among my treasures." Denny was playing in a trio with Ross Tompkins, piano player on *The Tonight Show*, and bassist John Heard the first time he heard Patitucci. They performed at the Long Beach Jazz Festival one year, probably around 1978, and Seiwell recalls there was this kid they couldn't get rid of, who just kept hanging around.

"Later that day we did our show, and he appeared as the bass player in the Long Beach University Big Band," Denny recalls. "He was probably 18 or 19 and that was John Patitucci."

The trio with Ross Tompkins and Russell George also played the Newport Jazz Festival with Anita O'Day. He recalls that she always wore white gloves, but somehow she ended up with only one, and she was in a tizzy. "We said, 'We don't care if you sing with one glove or no gloves, but you're going to sing," and she did with one glove, and it went very well."

There was another trio date at the Playboy Club with Ross Tompkins, but with bassist Monty Budwig, featuring singer Joe Williams. "Joe was a big deal at the time. I was a little too big for my britches and Joe was kinda an old-world singer. Instead of going spang-a-lang (as we call it), I kinda hipped it up a little and Joe turned around to me and made it clear he did not like it. That was the last time I ever did that. Whenever I play with any of the traditional singers or players, I'll just give it to them like it was. I've had a couple of valuable lessons like that over the years."

Jingle work was done for his buddy Richard Druz, who built a studio in his house in Beachwood Canyon. Druz hired Denny for such accounts as Mattel and Lays potato chips. He also worked for contractors Don Piestrup and Anthony Harris. Looking at his calendar book, Seiwell spots a day where one morning he was with Anthony Harris at A&M Studios from 11-12, then Richard Druz from 12-1:20 and then went to another studio for a jingle with Don Piestrup from 2-3. Another day was Anthony Harris from 10-12, Richard Druz from 12:30-2, and Don Piestrup from 2-4 at Bell Studios.

"That used to happen quite a bit," he says.

During 1981, Seiwell also worked with comedian Martin Mull, who he says was "funnier than hell." "I'll never forget doing a show at a gay club in San Francisco; he walked out on stage and said, 'I'm a little confused. I thought I was in Queens.'" The big gig, though, was playing four nights in a row at the Los Angeles Greek Theatre in June of 1981 with Mike Melvoin and Ed Weiss on keyboards, Bill Bodine on bass and Marty Pizzulo, Wendy Mull and Marie LeClerc on background vocals.

He was also playing with Darrell Leonard and the Lineup, an 18-piece big band with all the A-players in town. They played at the Blue Lagoon Saloon and at Malibu's Trancas Restaurant, where major acts would try their sets out in the '80s and '90s before heading out on the road. In that big band, Denny recalls the horns would line up in front of the stage and they performed what he describes as "NFL crunch-up music, with those plays in slow motion with rock 'n' roll music."

"One night at the Blue Lagoon Saloon (we played) upstairs, and I was still drinking pretty good. We had to pack up and carry our shit down the stairs and I was so drunk I just put my bass drum on the edge of the steps and kicked it and it just rolled down. That's the bass drum that's in the Hall of Fame in the Hard Rock in Cincinnati, Ohio."

FOUR SHEETS TO THE WIND

Sometime in the Spring of 1981, while McCartney was in town to record "The Girl is Mine" with Michael Jackson, he called Denny to come down to Westlake Recording Studios in West Hollywood to hang out. For that visit, he needed fortification, and he had a few drinks. He got to the studio before anyone else. He arrived at the designated time of 1:00, but as usual, the McCartneys showed up a couple of hours later. Denny sat in his car until he saw them pull into the parking lot and then got out and greeted them, "'Hey man.' They came over and gave me a big hug. I was pretty loaded. They could tell. I didn't know what else to do. We went inside. He put the whole film crew and Michael Jackson, and Quincy Jones on hold while we went into a little corner and sat down and talked for a while. It was a tough day."

After they made small talk, McCartney got up to join the session and Seiwell bailed.

SHELBY FLINT, ETC.

Shelby Flint Band poses for 30-year reunion shows in Los Angeles, circa 2015. L-R: Greg Karukas, Bill Bodine, Shelby Flint, Denny, Jerry Peterson, Jerry Steinholtz. (Courtesy of Shelby Flint)

Around 1982 Seiwell got a call from a keyboard player named Red Young. Denny had begun to work with an artist by the name of Shelby Flint, who was in the jazz-pop vein. She had a big hit called "Angel on My Shoulder" in her early 20s and became a studio singer. The Shelby Flint Group, consisting of Seiwell, Red Young, Bill Bodine, Gregg Karukas, Jerry Peterson, and Jerry Steinholtz released the LP *You've Been on My Mind*, recorded at Armin Steiner's Sound Labs. For a couple of years, the band was one of the biggest L.A. draws. They worked together for about five years, during which they played the Monterey Jazz Festival. Seiwell produced the last album with her, which was not released.

Jerry Peterson, who played with Flint, also played sax in Billy and the Beaters, so occasionally when their regular drummer couldn't make it, they called Seiwell to sub. Darrell Leonard, Billy Vera's trumpet player, had a big band and he would call Seiwell whenever his drummer couldn't make it as well.

A memorable project was a few tracks on Deniece Williams' 1983 *I'm So Proud* album. Seiwell recalls getting a call from "Philly" Billy Neale, a guitar player Denny describes as part of the Philadelphia sound. It was a project he felt proud of because it was with a group of players he not always got to record with.

"He was also part of the *Gong Show* band, and my friend Ray Neopolitan was part of that *Gong Show* band, too, for years. Ray would come out and say, 'Hey Chuckie, hey Chuckie, I got a song, I got a song,' and he'd start singing a song and you'd know it would start going into something dirty. He got a lot of airtime like that and became a personality on the show. Billy and Ray got very close, and I hung out with them a lot. So Billy got an album to produce for Deniece Williams who was an incredible talent. "Ready" Freddie Washington was on bass. It was so much fun."

That same year, he got a call from producer Brooks Arthur to record a tune by a Japanese artist named Junko Yagami.

"She was like the Olivia Newton-John of Japan. She had a string of hits. They were in town, and she wanted to record this ballad here. They had called every drummer in town and they just could not get this song the way they heard it. Brooks was an engineer/producer I had worked with in New York, and he knew ballads were kinda my thing, so he called me in. I had already heard that every drummer in town had been called in for this and they weren't happy with what they had. They finally got around to me, and I said to Brooks, 'Ya know Brooks, this is going to cost you a whole lot more money now because you put me at the end of the list.' I came in and I got it. They loved it and it was the one they used."

In 1986 Denny was in his early 40s and playing golf one day at Burbank's Lakeside Golf Club with DJ Rick Dees and his golf caddie Fitz. Both of them had just hit sand trap shots out of hole 16.

"I'll never forget it, from the sand trap into the hole for birdies. I was blown away. They had a deal that if one of them got a hole in one on a par 3, it was an instant $1,000 whip out and they did. But that day, I went into the bar with them, and I remember feeling this chest pain, kinda like a tightness in my chest. I had a couple of beers and relaxed and it went away."

The next day Seiwell was in a studio in Santa Monica, and he felt the pains in his chest again, but a little more pronounced. He called Dr. Gold, who told him he'd better see Dr. Steve Beren. They couldn't take any chances. After all, Denny's lifestyle of alcohol and drugs could have put his heart in danger, not to mention the fact that Seiwell says he had been a very heavy smoker ("If I was awake and breathing, I was smoking"). The fact that his father had died of a heart attack at the age of 57 also contributed to his worrisome health profile.

On November 26, 1986, on Thanksgiving and Denny and Monique's 20th anniversary, Seiwell went into the cath lab to undergo an angioplasty under local anesthesia. He was awake while Dr. Beren checked to see what was going on in his heart and found a massive blockage in one of his arteries.

"This was before stents," Seiwell explains. "So he said, 'What we're going to do is put a balloon in there and inflate it and it is going to squash all the gook up against the walls and then we will give you diets and such so it will stay open. It will be up to you to keep it open. We're getting the balloon in place now.' And as he's saying that, the nurse said, 'He's going, he's going, he's gone.'"

Denny actually heard the nurse say those words. They told him later that they had to paddle him to bring him back to life. He was in the hospital for a couple of days and nights and recalls that he was laid in bed between two boards—one underneath and one on top, taped very tight—to keep pressure on the procedure where they had gone into the groin to put the camera into the heart and look around.

When the doctor came in to tell Seiwell he could go home, he asked, "What can I do and what can't I do?" He said: "You can never do cocaine again." Denny replied, "I don't need that; I don't like it anyway. What about marijuana?" "Well, a study just came out that says it speeds up the heart rate." "Okay, I'll be careful. What about alcohol?" The doctor said, "There's just been a study that says a glass of white wine a day is good for circulation."

When his friend Ray Neapolitan, who owned a limo company, sent a limo to pick him up from the hospital, Denny asked the driver to make two stops: one at his dope dealer's house for a little bag of weed, and one to Vendome Liquor for two bottles of white wine. For the next five years Denny behaved himself. He had one glass of white wine a day and a puff off the joint once in a while. He ate nothing but chicken, fish and vegetables, drank decaffeinated coffee and ran around Lake Hollywood every morning. But after a while the disease of alcohol resumed its nasty hold over Denny with its usual excuses, "This time it'll be different, you'll respect King Alcohol this time."

RESIDUALS TAVERN

Residuals Tavern opened in 1986 on Ventura Blvd. in Studio City with the gimmick that if you brought in a residual check with the sum of 50 cents or less, they poured you a free drink. Craig Tennis, the former talent coordinator at *The Tonight Show*, managed the club.

"One day I was in the bar having a drink and he said, 'Do you want to bring in some music? We've been thinking about trying some music in here. Let's try bringing some jazz in here on Sunday nights. But I don't want your ordinary jazz; I want something a little unique.' I thought about it for a minute and said, 'How does this sound: bassoon, accordion and drums?' He said, 'What???' I said, 'Yeah, Ray Pizzi—'The Pizza Man'—plays a mean bassoon and Frank Marocco is the best accordion player in the world. You don't need any more than that; that's music right there. I'll just hang on for dear life. We'll bring some jazz in there.' It was incredible. At one point Frank hurt his hand somehow, and I had to replace him with two people: Jim Fox on guitar and a bass player named John Leitham, who later became Jennifer Leitham, and who I worked with in the studios a lot and had actually worked with way back with Eartha Kitt. Today Jennifer is a major jazz star in the L.A. area. John had a line that was very funny when people asked him who he was working with. He responded, 'Eartha Kitt…some assembly required!'"

After a while, the manager suggested they try Brazilian music, so Denny hired Brazilian guitarist/singer Kleber Jorge. After that, Tennis decided rock 'n' roll might be an even bigger draw, so Seiwell hired Sweet Grease, the blues band he had been doing some casuals with singer Maurice Miller, Dwayne Smith on electric piano, and Davey Faragher on vocals and bass.

"It went over immediately," Denny says. "I was drinking quite a bit. We played two or three sets a night every Saturday night and that went on for some six years. It became an institution. If anyone came through town, they came in and sat in, like Bernard Purdie came in. We were good friends. He helped me get started in New York just by being so busy. They'd say, 'Get the white kid who plays like Purdie, but smiles.' When Bernard came in, he said, 'Do you guys know, 'More Than You'll Ever Know' (written by Al Kooper, sung by Donny Hathaway), and I thought, 'Oh my God, he made that record, too?' It is the slowest tempo—you can get loaded between the counts. Neal Schon came in, Steve Lukather came in and played a couple of times. Ginger Baker came in one time. They were really great times."

VOICEOVERS

For years, Denny would be on sessions and producers would say to him, "You've got a really good voice, you should do voiceovers." When the work began to slow down in 1985, he took a couple of classes. A woman by the name of Vanessa Gilbert, whom he had met in 1974 at the Joe Cocker session in London, was a voiceover agent at a company called Talent Group and she took him on as a client. Another one of her clients was percussionist Joe Lala.

"The two of us would go down to Talent Group together and she would show us the copy, and we would go into the stairway and smoke a joint and work on it. The business was pretty demanding. They had regular people they worked with and there was a certain amount of loyalty; once you got an account, they would call you back for it. There was a guy I met later in the program who was doing a TV show called *The Lazarus Man* at a little studio near Capitol and he asked me to read for him: 'Tonight, the mystery of the Lazarus Man continues,'" Denny says, in a deep mysterious voice. "And he said, 'Wow, you can do this shit, man,' so he gave me the job, and for a couple of years, I'd go in there for 15 minutes and they gave me a 10-second, 15-second, 30-second and 60-second spot. I'd do the 60-second spot and I'd get that within the first five minutes, and they'd cut it into the other spots. Here I am getting checks."

At Talent Group there was a woman married to artist Paul Williams who asked if Denny did any on-camera work. She had a Harley Davidson ad to cast for which she thought he'd be perfect. Gilbert asked him if he was interested, and he said sure. They told him not to shave for about a week, wear tattered jeans, and they shot the catalog clothing ad at the beach with a notable New York model.

"We shot it down in Huntington Beach for two or three days; I had a ball and did it for two years in a row. The following year they called and wanted to dress me up like an executive. I had long hair, they let me shave, but they put a shirt and tie on with a leather jacket and boots, and I carried a Harley Davidson briefcase. It was shot in the desert up near Edwards Air Force Base in a little mining camp. I got to ride on the back of a Harley with a sunset across the desert with a guy who was a real biker from Milwaukee who was in the shoot as well. He put me on the back, and we were doing 130 miles an hour against the setting sun in the desert and it was just gorgeous. I dug that. It was cool."

Several years later, his agent called him to ask if he wanted to do an actual on-camera corporate commercial for GM. Seiwell really didn't like it, but he did it because work was slow. He was booked on a Cadillac commercial and drove up to Santa Maria, where they put him in some Banana Republic clothing, did his make-up, and then they took him to the set where the hood of the Cadillac STS was open.

"The director said to me, 'We want you to look at the engine like it's a beautiful woman and caress the engine as if it were breasts,'" Seiwell recalls with a laugh.

"I'm laughing my ass off and said, 'Are you fucking serious?' She said, 'Yes. Give it your best shot.' I was there for 10 minutes. They filmed me opening up the hood of this STS Cadillac and admiring the engine. I drove home thinking, 'Nothing will come of it; just another thing to make a buck.' About a month or two later, my agent called and said, 'Get yourself down to the office, you've got a shitload of money.' It started coming in. It was a Class A national spot. I never saw the commercial; a lot of people did. It would come in $1500 checks and there'd be a stack of them sometimes. Then it went from Class A to Spanish, and then it went corporate. It ran for close to three years. I got at least $50,000 or $60,000, and I was able to get insurance through Screen Actors Guild, so it paid for my knee replacements in 2003 and 2004."

WITH A LITTLE HELP FROM MY FRIENDS

At the beginning of 1990 Denny was drinking a lot. He had two watering holes: the Casting Office and Residuals. Craig Tennis, the manager at Residuals, didn't charge him to drink because he was providing the music. What a kind gift for an alcoholic.

Sometime in September of that year, while following his regular routine of showing up at the Casting Office in Studio City when they opened at 10:40 a.m. with his burrito and ordering a beer, he started to notice that his regular drinking buddy, notable actor/comedian, Sandy Baron, was drinking pineapple juice and coffee.

"He'd hang out at the bar and have little wads of paper in his pocket to remember little bits for his comedy act. I said, 'What the hell, Sandy, you got sober.' And he said, 'Yeah, I'm going to meetings.' So I asked him to take me to the Comedy Store, where they had meetings. He said, 'Sure, you'll feel right at home. It stinks of stale beer and cigarettes.' I walked in and there were about 15 or 20 people, nobody was sitting next to one another. There was someone on stage running the meeting and they were going to have a speaker, and the guy was a trumpet player I knew. He was sober five years. I don't remember much about it, but I remember feeling good about walking into this place where my nightmare might be over."

Sandy Baron is what is considered in the alcoholics' jargon to be Seiwell's "eskimo": the one to lead him out of the cold into the program.

After that, Denny didn't drink. He would go down to the Casting Office and hang out and get a cup of coffee or a Coke, but no alcohol. Right around that time, the guy who ran Residuals called and asked him to go by there, so he began making the rounds from the Casting Office to Residuals, one after the other, but he refrained from drinking.

Although Seiwell had stopped drinking alcohol in 1990, he didn't realize that being sober encompassed all substances, so he was still smoking marijuana. When he finally realized that fact during a meeting one night at the end of 1990, he planned for New Year's Eve and New Year's Day to be his last hurrah. As of Jan 2, 1991, Seiwell has been completely sober. In the beginning, he attended a few meetings a day, afraid he would slip.

During his first month, he attended a convention for the program, and he met a man he had heard speak at some of the meetings. Denny introduced himself and asked if he would help him. He said he would and that's when Seiwell really felt like everything began to turn around for him.

"He was a comedy writer and very funny," Seiwell says. "His name was Scott Redman, and he wrote the book called *Real Men Don't Cook Quiche*. He really guided me into the program and showed me how to stay sober. He became my spiritual advisor who got me onboard with the 12 steps, and he did it in such a beautiful way, because he did it with humor. One son played drums, one son played piano, and Scott played guitar. I was at the house once and saw they had a set of drums, and I got behind it and started playing. They were all sitting on the couch and the minute I started playing, they were airborne; it was so cute. He got me going and helped me look at things that were bothering me, like the huge resentment I had about not getting paid with McCartney, and the reasons I drank. Through that whole process I was able to own my issues and then make amends for them and then get on with my life. He was very instrumental. And because of the way he knew and worked the program, I started doing that for others. I could see the rewards, and today, 30, 40 years later, I am the spiritual advisor for at least 20 guys at any given moment."

"A man of service," is how Denny describes Redman and as a terrific cook, he would always volunteer to provide his talents for the group on Thanksgiving and Christmas. "He was a beautiful guy that everyone loved and respected. He would speak at all the world conventions, and he became an authority on the program. It was a beautiful accident that I was able to hook up with him and he got me on my way," Denny says, explaining that he helped him connect spiritually with God and people going through the same thing. "After that, it got real easy because I had a fellowship around me; not just a bunch of drunks at a bar."

Denny says it was actually a lot of fun without alcohol. Even though he had never played impaired, he always had performed with alcohol in his system. He remembers the first time he ever played drums completely sober.

"It was a Saturday night at Residuals with Sweet Grease, a band I had with Maurice Miller, a singer who had been with the Fifth Dimension, a blind piano player, Dwayne Smith, and a great bass player named Davey Faragher who still plays with Elvis Costello. After a year or so we hired a guitar player who would sit in, Miles Joseph.

"Every night when we'd go to work it was, go out in the alley, smoke a joint, do a couple of toots, go in and have a couple of drinks and then play," Denny continues. "The first night I was sober, instead of going out in the alley, I sat down behind my drums and said a little prayer, thanking God for what He left me in my life.

Denny says that first time playing without any substance in his body was great. "I knew there was nothing between me and the music. I was so grateful that I could do that. Everything is better. They say that in the program: 'Everything is better when you're sober: taking a crap is better, having sex is better, eating food is better. Everything.'"

"The bass player had been sober, and we recommended one another for sessions and one day I asked him, 'Davey, what was it really like those last couple of years before I got sober?' He said, 'The first set you were fucking great. The second set you were a little weird and the third set you were all over the place.'" Recovery made that all go away, and good things started to happen.

Monique at His Master's Wheels for the *Mallory Earl* TV program shoot, 1975. (Photo by Pat Stewart)

NOW A WORD FROM MY BETTER HALF... MONIQUE

MONIQUE'S STORY

Leaving Nice at 18 and living in London as an au pair was freedom for Monique. She went to the university to learn English; she was good about attending classes at first but then realized she really didn't need the grammar as much as she needed to learn conversational English. She had already learned the grammar from the nuns at school in France, where English was a requirement.

"I realized I wasn't very good at conversation, so I took to the street," Monique says, explaining she spent time with the British kids. "When I went back to France four years later—it was only supposed to be a year, but it was too much of a good time, so I stayed four years—so at the end of '64 I went back to Nice and started to hang out with English, American and Swedish kids so I could keep up my English."

Monique didn't have a career in mind, but knew she wasn't interested in French men. She found them aggressive and controlling and found American men more respectful.

"I wasn't looking to get married; I was enjoying myself," Monique says.

But the first thing she felt when she met Denny was comfort. "It was easy and comfortable, and he was respectful and I liked to be with him."

Looking back, she thinks it was love at first sight. It felt different from anything before. It took her a little off guard. "I got caught," she says.

Monique found Denny's ambition very appealing—the fact that he had a vision and was actively pursuing it. America was also attractive; her sense of adventure was calling her. She had never been to the States. She was ready for a new adventure, although their first stop in Pennsylvania was, as she puts it, a little limited. Monique found a job at a new boutique in Allentown and actually really enjoyed it. It was 1966, and it was very trendy.

"And I knew we weren't staying there; that it was just a transition, and I liked that too. It was just temporary," Monique says.

They moved a lot after that—the Catskills, the Poconos—and Monique would ask: "How long, how long this time?"

Eventually they landed in Manhattan and Monique felt as though they had arrived.

But their first apartment on 91st Street was filled with cockroaches. "I remember pulling the refrigerator away from the wall to clean and it was black with cockroaches. They were running this way and that way. It was horrible."

They didn't stay long. Their next apartment was on 69th Street and thankfully it was better. Denny began to get busy, and Monique got a job at a management company as a receptionist. They trained her and she loved it.

She remembers being very excited when she was hired by a French perfume company on Madison Avenue after that and much to her disappointment, Denny came home to tell her they needed to pack their bags to go to Los Angeles. "But I knew getting married to him would be an adventure, and I loved that. So, with Denny, anything could happen, and it was more important for him to get ahead, and whatever he needed to do, I would follow."

Monique was happy when they were on their way back to New York on that infamous cross-country car trip with Joe Beck and his friend Ginger. Back in New York, Monique got a job as a secretary for an educational book publishing company that sent books to India. She had taken courses in shorthand, so despite the fact that she had no clue what they were talking about in their meetings, she took the minutes. "I bullshitted my way through that and stayed two or three years until McCartney."

And during the time Denny was playing at the supper club, sometimes Monique would go to work, come home, change her clothes and take a cab to go see Denny play at night.

One day, Denny came home and told her that he had auditioned for Paul McCartney. "It wasn't like, 'Oh my God, you have to get it,'" Monique recalls. "He had lots of work. I asked him what it was like, though. When he called me to tell me he had gotten the job to do the album, I picked up a small bottle of champagne on my way home from the office."

It was really just another job; Denny had already done albums with big stars, and they didn't know that it was going to go beyond the album. Denny did invite Monique to the session one day, so after work she went down to Columbia Studio. She recalls walking in and not wanting to gawk at the McCartneys, she concentrated on little Mary.

"They probably thought I was a future mom and loved babies. Maybe that's why they asked me to go on tour. They were very warm and welcoming."

During the making of the album there were a couple of aforementioned dinners.

They had moved from 69th to 68th Street, and after the box of records arrived and when McCartney called and invited them to Scotland, the Seiwells still didn't know how their future was about to change. When McCartney asked Denny to be part of a band with him, it was a no-brainer for Denny. He didn't really ask Monique, but that wasn't really part of the relationship; it was about Denny's career.

They kept the apartment in New York for a little while, but eventually they had to let it go. And Monique did love London, so it was fine. They were living on a shoestring, but Monique recalls it was the time of second-hand store shopping and they managed to furnish whatever place they rented and buy clothing on whatever funds they had.

Of course, there was the other side of it. On tour there were the fancy hotels, chefs cooking them special meals, private jets, gala parties, celebrities galore. It wasn't that Monique was starstruck or that impressed, but it did create another side to the day to day struggle the couple had when they were off the road.

She had become an integral part of the touring unit because Linda relied on her to watch the kids when Rose, the official nanny, wasn't there. She would watch the kids while they were onstage. Monique notes that Linda was under a lot of pressure and while she knew there was an underlying friendship between the two of them, it wasn't visible on the road.

"The write-ups about her were so unkind," Monique says. In hindsight, Monique realizes that Linda couldn't let her guard down because she probably had to stand tall in the face of all the criticism surrounding her part in Wings. "If I had realized all that, I would have been more compassionate. I did admire her for what she was doing; I couldn't have done what she was doing. She did suffer, though."

Throughout Denny's time in Wings, the Seiwells talked about the difficult financial arrangements, but when the straw finally broke the camel's back after the European tour, Monique says she listened to her husband as he made that difficult phone call to McCartney to leave the band. When he got off the phone, Monique gave Denny a big kiss to let him know she was standing beside him.

When they returned to New York after those couple of months when Denny worked some freelance recording sessions in London, Monique called her old job where she had been a secretary to ask if, by chance, they needed her. And lo and behold, the timing was great; they said, "Come on back!" Denny was in New York for a little bit before he put that band together with Henry McCullough and the West Coast and Chicago adventure occurred, beginning the dark chapter in the Seiwell marriage.

Denny was dealing with an identity crisis, coming down from what he felt would be the greatest moment of his life, never to be matched again. How would he get back on top? Monique was fighting to move on; to move ahead without looking back.

While Monique remained in New York and spoke to Denny on the phone, it seemed strained. She knew he was going through a tough time and their communication felt burdensome and forced for the first time in their marriage. Monique remained steadfast and believed they would somehow get through this terrible time.

Through the San Francisco and L.A. chapters, just as in New York, Monique concentrated on work. The couple moved to the West Coast in 1975 and while Denny was contributing income to the household, the couple considers Monique to have been the real breadwinner as she climbed the ladder at Wells Fargo Bank from receptionist in 1979 to Vice President in the late '90s. Her nickname as the V.P. was "the Queen of the Impossible," and she headed loans for major developers, finally retiring in 2008.

She recalls one episode where she was at a seminar in San Francisco for the bank she worked at and suddenly she heard someone say, "What is she doing here? Her husband was with Paul McCartney!"

"I thought, 'Oh fuck!' I didn't move, I didn't say anything. It was somebody I didn't know, but somebody must have told her." The implication was I didn't need a job because Denny had worked for McCartney, even though Monique had never told a soul.

One day after that, a few of the loan officers were gathered around a computer as she walked in early in the morning. She saw they were looking at a photo of the McCartneys, Denny and her with baby Stella in her arms. "Is that you?" they asked. "Yes," she said. "That was then and this is now," and she walked to her desk, making it clear that this would be the end of the conversation. She never wanted her personal life to be in the way of her work life. Work kept her going.

Once the Seiwells got to L.A., Denny's drinking began to wear on Monique more and more and her self-preservation truly was her work. "Looking back, I know that saved me. I couldn't lose my job. It covered the insurance for both of us. I had to focus, and I stayed at my work until 7:00 because I didn't want to go home."

The drinking got worse. Monique would get home and Denny would be gone. She became so focused on putting one foot in front of the other, that she reflects now that she probably appeared cold and hard to outsiders as Denny fell lower and lower. In fact, she remembers one time taking him to an appointment to get his heart checked. "I dropped him there and took off. A lot of people might have thought it was not nice," Monique says.

But that way of dealing with things was the only way she knew how to get through the pain of living with an alcoholic: remaining stoic and impenetrable, never allowing herself the luxury to fall apart. Except one time as they drove across the Golden Gate Bridge. Denny recalls, she had one hand on the car handle to jump out. "I felt that every time we were on that bloody bridge," she confesses. "In my mind, I was going to do it *today*."

But she emphasizes that work saved their relationship and her life. "And I gladly took all the shit at work."

And all the while she worked, Denny drank and there was no communication, and if there was, it was not good communication. If he would start talking about how the McCartney situation let him down, Monique would say,

"Aren't you over that yet," neither one realizing how deep their isolation was hurting them. "I didn't know. He kept it in. And I couldn't talk to him about my work either, so we were both in the same situation."

Monique remembers getting in the car at night after a fight to look for her husband. She would go to one of the bars he frequented and see him getting into his car and think, "Oh good, he's going home," only to watch him pass the house and drive to the next bar.

She confesses she packed her bag one time. She walked down the stairs and out to the street, but couldn't do it. She walked back into the house and that was that.

When Denny faced the heart problem, he knew his drinking days were numbered, but it was still several years before he actually quit. And Monique kept just focusing on her work, perhaps looking like "a cold-hearted bitch," she says, but preserving her sanity.

She was extremely irked when they would have to attend her work functions and Denny would say, "Why do we have to?" "I would think, 'You ungrateful prick, this is what saved us!' Nobody at my job knew why I would stay at my job until 7:00 at night. I had finished all my work, but there was nothing to go home to."

Both of them felt alone and separate and didn't know how to stop it or fix it, but they never threw in the towel.

Monique started to see the littlest change as Denny's new friend, comedian Sandy Baron, took him to a recovery meeting. Seeds began to plant for Denny, but very slowly.

"He kept telling me this guy he met—a great guy (his first sponsor) —was going to help."

They went to a Thanksgiving event, and it was encouraging. Denny had just gotten sober, and she felt hope. There were potluck dinners, and they began to associate with a different group of people.

"With time I began to see changes in Denny." It began to make big changes in their relationship. "And I was included in what he was doing. I wasn't left at home while he went drinking. I went with him, and I was part of his life. I could see he was serious—finally."

When Denny got sober, Monique says they forgave each other, but they did not "go on about it. We became nicer to each other and really didn't bring it up much."

The heaviness was also eased when the settlement from McCartney came. They purchased their Woodland Hills home in 2002 and sought financial advice when Monique received her 401(k) payout upon her retirement.

In retrospect, both are so grateful that they made it through the heartbreak to the other side.

MAKING AMENDS

The tenet of the recovery program is to apologize to all those one hurt while under the spell of substance abuse. Denny says (with a little laugh) all these years later he's *still* making amends to Monique. In all seriousness though, he explains he may not have sat down with her first; he may have chosen a few people for which he had far less to apologize on whom to practice first.

He explains the amends aren't just in the words said, they are in actions made. "Every time I went to a meeting, every time I talked to another guy, every time I followed the practice of recovery, it was a form of making amends."

Seiwell believes between 1993 and 1996, he both called and wrote McCartney with amends. He remembers, while on one of the film dates, that he began writing the letter, trying to explain how he felt. "I'll never forget writing that I was on a big orchestra date for a film and that I wanted to take the time to tell him how sorry I was for the way I left the band and left him in the lurch and should have instead sat down and talked about it."

In April 1993 the Seiwells caught wind of McCartney's concert at Angel Stadium in Anaheim. Since it was in the midst of McCartney's world tour, Denny had no way to reach him, so he and Monique decided to just take a ride down to the venue.

"We went behind the stadium, and I saw a security guard and I said, 'Hey, when you go in again, could you just go into McCartney's dressing room, could you tell him Denny and Monique are out here. I was the original drummer with Wings.' He went in and came out on a golf cart 30 seconds later and said, 'Hop on.' We were ushered right into the dressing room, and there were Paul and Linda and the three kids."

Linda told the kids it was wonderful to see us again and gave Denny all their various contact numbers with the parting message: "Let's stay in touch."

Denny still had the house number in London and the house in Scotland, but

Denny on the hood of his 1962 B18 round back Volvo in front of his parents' home. (Photo by Monique Seiwell)

now there was another way to get in touch. A few years later the cell phone entered the picture, and McCartney contacted him via cell. Denny made note of that number and then Paul mentioned that he should send messages via MPL, his office in London; Denny felt as though that was somewhat of a step backwards, but it really wasn't.

"I would have to go to him every time to get permission to use something on an album of mine," Seiwell says. "I would go through the girl at the office to get to him. And then there would be bad news about someone passing away and Paul and I would have a conversation about it and pretty soon we were talking about things that mattered. Then we spoke about the *Wingspan* project (2001)."

But before that, on April 17, 1998, Linda passed away. Denny and Monique were invited to the memorial service held for her on June 23, 1998, at Riverside Church in New York City, which they attended.

"I thought we were going to sit at the back of the church, and they wouldn't even know we were there, but when we got there, they had somebody usher us right up to the front of the church," Denny reveals. "They seated us in a pew right across from the family."

At that moment, Denny felt his amends had been accepted.

In August 1999, Paul held another memorial service in London called "A Garland for Linda," to which the Seiwells were invited. They attended the service, which was quite elaborate and videoed for release in October 2000.

Either late 1999 or early 2000, McCartney invited Denny down to the House of Blues to see him play with drummer Ian Paice and guitarist David Gilmour. Paul had just released the *Run Devil Run* album.

"He invited me to the Foundation Room, the private room at the House of Blues. I told him I could come to the sound check, but I couldn't stay for the show; I had something else going on that night. So, I was standing in the Foundation Room and there were just four people standing in the room: Paul McCartney, Phil Everly, Brian Wilson and me. We're standing in a little group in the middle of the room, and it's rock 'n' roll history. I just kept my mouth shut and drooled. And then at one point, Brian began to talk about Linda and suddenly a guy from the back who had been listening, Brian Wilson's therapist, walked up and tapped Brian on the shoulder and said, 'We're not going to talk about Linda today,' and then the shrink backed off again. It was a pretty wild moment in time."

Not long after "A Garland for Linda," Denny and Monique went to London to see how Paul was doing and to ask him if he might want to put Wings together for a reunion in conjunction with Recording Artists and Actors and Athletes Against Drunk Driving to benefit Linda's food company. McCartney was keen on the idea and suggested Denny check with the other band members. They all agreed, but when Denny returned to Paul with the news, Paul said he realized he would not be able to perform with Wings without Linda; that it would be like putting the Beatles back together without John.

It was during that visit in 2000 that McCartney told Denny that they were going to make a documentary about Wings and reissue all the music from the beginning on forward. Denny asked Paul what he could do to help. "He asked for some footage I had, which I gave him," Seiwell recalls. "Then I called my buddy at the record company and said, 'I see a lot of promo on this thing. If people bought this music 30 years ago, why would they buy it again?' And he said, 'I'm not sure, but we're shipping two million units.' I thought, 'Oh no, I can't let this money go by again.'"

RECONCILIATION

Despite the amends, there had not been a true reconciliation between Denny and Paul. And yet, Denny and McCartney kept reaching out even though things were still unsettled. Denny ponders: "We had something so special. He knew it; I knew it. He would track me down and reach out." But McCartney never broached the subject with him; he never confronted the elephant in the room. He never asked Denny why, and Denny continued to put on a face of being the successful session musician, impervious to the situation. And in the real world, thankfully, he was able to put that face on, too, and do the work that has earned him a living and given him a retirement.

When his sponsor at the time, Steve T., first suggested he sit down and write

Denny, Monique and Paul at Hoghill Studio, Paul's studio in the South of England, 1999. (Photo by John Hammel)

McCartney a letter, Denny recalls, "I said to him, 'I can't. I just made a deal with God: 'If you keep me from drinking, I don't care if I ever see a penny from those days.'" He said a beautiful thing: 'You gotta remember, God's old and He moves slow.'"

Denny sat down and wrote a letter. He wrote three drafts, attempting to write it in the most loving way possible, and he read it to Steve.

"I said, 'I've got to remind you of a few things: This is what was promised to me, this is what I got, and this is what I felt.' I told him about the meeting with Brian Brolley where he gave me a check at the Beverly Wilshire Hotel in 1975 which was supposed to be my payoff for almost three years with Wings. I sent the letter and upon receiving it, Paul read it and that's when he called me in tears and said, 'I'm so sorry; I had no idea.' At that point I began dealing with his financial officer, Paul Wynn, who sent me another ridiculously low offer. I told him, 'If Paul is trying to do the right thing, let him do the right thing.'"

They finally offered Seiwell an acceptable settlement along with an NDA in which he agreed not to disclose the amount to anyone.

"I'm imagining this, of course, but I believe that Paul got the letter and with the letter in one hand, he read it and picked up the phone with the other hand and called me. And he was in tears, and he said, 'I'm so sorry. I had no idea that my business people rolled over you.' I had nothing to show for the three years I was in Wings, which was a pretty big deal, after having been offered a slice of the pie. We talked for a few minutes and he said, 'I'm going to make this right.' Then I called Niq at work and said, 'You're never going to believe what just happened. Paul read the letter, he called me in tears and said he was going to make it right.' And she screamed like she had gotten the news that someone in the family had died. Everybody in the office stopped and asked, 'What is going on?' It was that major. I knew in my heart of hearts it was because of the (spiritual) work I was doing. There was a ton of relief."

The first check arrived in March 2001, and it definitely took the edge off the resentment. The first time Denny saw his old boss after the settlement was at Paul's Los Angeles Staples Center show in October 2002. Denny doesn't remember much about it, except standing in line waiting to see McCartney in the star-studded backstage area, but the outing ended up being completely uneventful.

Seiwell next saw McCartney in 2007 with his new band consisting of Abe

Paul and Denny having some fun at McCartney's Hoghill Studio in the South of England. (Photo by John Hammel)

Laboriel, Jr.; Brian Ray; Rusty Anderson and Wix Wickens, when they played a show at the Amoeba Record Store on Sunset Blvd. in Hollywood.

"We're all standing there (and I was standing next to Ringo Starr, who is a friend), and Paul with his new band played a Beatles song. Of course, Abe did really well, God bless him—he had to play in front of Ringo! But I turned to Ringo and said, 'Why aren't you up there?' And he gave me one of those looks like, 'Yeah, really,' And a minute later, they did a Wings song, and Ringo turned to me and said, 'Why aren't you up there?' It was almost comical. He's playing with this new band in a record store, and we were standing right in front of him. The fans would have gone fucking crazy! I could never figure that out."

GIVING GOD A HAND

By January 1992 Seiwell had completed all 12 steps. "I had done a complete inventory; I had owned my part in all the shit."

Denny explained that the inventory part of the process was the fourth step. "It's a moral inventory where you look at your resentments, your fears and your sexual problems. You try to spot the character defects in yourself that caused you to have this problem with drugs or alcohol. By owning those character defects and fears, you can talk to your higher power about changing your behavior. By owning your part in it that caused the resentment, you can also get to the place where you can forgive that person. After you've looked at yourself like that, they say in the program you've swallowed some big chunks of truth about yourself."

It was a several-month internal journey, but Denny started feeling really good early on in the sobriety. He had no idea that it would bring up so much that after the inventory process, he would feel like a new human being. He had to figure out what exactly to do with his life. His hope was to reestablish himself as one of the premium session players in Los Angeles, which is what he came to the West Coast to do. But by the 1990s the landscape of recording was changing with Pro Tools, digital, samples and even some home recording. So, he decided maybe it was time to try something else. He had to put his life in

God's hands. There was a point when he said to God, "If you don't want me to do music anymore, I'm good with that. Whatever you want me to do, I'm good with that. I just don't want to drink again." He began to look for a job, put on a suit and tie and went to a sales job interview in Beverly Hills.

"There was nothing on my resume but music," Denny says. "I did the interview and came out of there feeling so hopelessly depressed. I asked God, 'Please don't make me do this, but if you want me to, please send me the job and I'll do it.' The minute I got home, the phone rang, and it was my friend Richard Bennett, who had been the guitar player for Neil Diamond. Whenever they wanted someone different, they would call me in to do demos with them down at Neil's studio on 3rd Street; it was gorgeous. He called me from Nashville where he had relocated. He said, 'Hey, my regular guy isn't available and I have a session booked with this guy David Ball. Would you come down and do this record with me?' And I said 'Fuck yeah!' The timing was so great because I was ready to just give up music."

Although the album never came out, for Seiwell, it just reassured his faith that he was on the right track.

Because he was sober now, he was more accepting. His attitude was, "I'm not going to fight it; I'm just going to do as much as I can."

"There were moments that were disheartening," he admits. "Like, 'Why did I do all this, and I still can't…' Monique worked at the bank. She started as a receptionist, became a secretary and worked her way up to vice president of a construction lending and she was making good money. We lived frugally. Some months I would do nothing and other months I would do very well, so it was difficult, but I handled it differently. Rather than go to the bar and pound down a bunch of booze, I had faith that everything was going to work out, as it did.

"I always tried to give God a hand with me, because I'm a handful," Denny continues with a laugh. "In recovery I thought, 'How can I give God a hand with me, so I'm less of a problem with him?' I would think of things to do, like teaching. At one point I had as many as 10 students a week—all the way from someone new to the drums to a professional. I was making money and I could contribute to the household expenses and feel good about myself and

L-R: Drum Workshop co-owner Don Lombardi, Denny, Denny's first student Zach Peck, mom Cheryl Tiegs, dad Tony Peck, DW co-owner John Good. (All rights reserved.)

people could learn more about playing drums."

Seiwell's very first student was Zack Peck, around 1999. Zach was probably 12 and he was the grandson of Gregory Peck. Denny knew Zach's father Tony, who had been married to his mother Cheryl Tiegs at the time.

"We were invited to the Peck's house for a Sunday afternoon picnic, and I remember walking in and there were 30 or 40 people. There was a long table. There was a priest there, a few celebs and we walked into the backyard and Gregory Peck came over to greet us and he put his arm around Monique, and I thought she was going to pass out. The only other time we met Gregory Peck (which I reminded him of) was at the film premiere in London of *Live and Let Die*. He had a tuxedo that was charcoal gray velvet. It was stunning, and when he walked into the room, heads turned. I reminded him of it, and he remembered. His wife, Veronique, was French, and they aren't known for being incredibly outgoing at first, but after a few years of teaching Zach, going to the house where the lesson was set up, we began to be invited for Thanksgiving dinners and Christmas dinners and such. We'd go around the table and say what we were grateful for, and Monique and I would sweat all the way down there, hoping we wouldn't say anything stupid in front of these people. After a while, Veronique warmed up and we became very close."

Through the years of their association with the Pecks, they sat in the company of so many greats, like Sidney Portier, Louis Jordan and Harry Belafonte. And what began as the transactional relationship of Seiwell providing lessons for a young drum student became a deep friendship. Denny says they felt a great loss when both Gregory and Veronique Peck passed on.

Actor/writer Tony Peck and Denny began working together in around 2007 on a screenplay on comedian Sandy Baron that they began before Gregory Peck died.

"We would go over to the house and into his study. Here I was, sitting with Gregory Peck's son, in his study, with all these first edition books like *Moby Dick* lining the walls."

When they completed it, they went through proper channels to register it with the Screen Actor's Guild and the Writer's Guild. When he went to a writer's conference in Nashville where he and producer Stewart Levine were the only two music related participants among all the attendees, he found all the writing-related folks wanted to hang out with the two of them.

"We got to meet a lot of people there and I met a woman from CAA (Creative Artists Agency), the top person who handled new projects. I had a lot in common with her and I sent her the script and she loved it; she said it was very good. She explained that they couldn't really get behind it at the time because of the script that had just come out with Jamie Foxx playing the homeless guy who played the cello downtown (*The Soloist*). In giving God a hand with my life, I've opened a lot of doors that are still open today."

Sandy Baron's agent recently revisited the script, and they have reimagined it with an additional writer.

RECOVERY PICNIC

While lending his talent playing with Dr. John at a program recovery picnic in 1995 at Calimigos Ranch in Malibu, Seiwell enjoyed a musical highlight. There were about 5,000 people in attendance, and Dr. John was the closing act of the day. After the closing act, Eric Clapton was to be the speaker about his experiences with recovery. Having rehearsed the night before, Seiwell went up to play with Dr. John and the band, which included the Tower Power Horns, some singers—about a ten-piece band.

"Dr. John—Mac (Malcolm John Rebennack)—turned around and saw Clapton standing over there listening, waiting to speak. So, Mac said, 'Come on Eric, you don't gets to keep it if you don't gives it away,' and Eric strapped on a guitar and played the whole set with us."

Seiwell speaks of recovery from addiction all over the world, in person or over Zoom, to audiences small and large, filled with addicts who have been sober one day or fifty years, about what he's learned from his own journey. He is so grateful to the program for saving his life that he believes it's his responsibility to help others as others have helped him, to give back and to pay it forward.

His messages are about how the program worked in his life, what happened in his life and what it's like now. "I talk about the lack of alcoholism in my family, what brought it on, what it was like, what happened, how I got tired of it, how I came to the decision to stop it and get sober and what my life is like now that I am sober. It (the program) *is* my life. Without it I wouldn't have had a life the past 30-plus years."

He has spoken at program meetings, schools, and even at a conference of 4,000 people involved in the criminal justice system that included judges, attorneys and rehabilitation personnel. He tailor-made his talk to show that the program works in order to keep an addict from having to be incarcerated for a drug offense.

"The guy who ran the organization West Huddleston CEO NAADCP was a guy I met at the meeting who liked what I talked about and asked me to come and speak."

Denny relays one comical experience when he was put up in a five-star hotel in Boston to be a keynote speaker. The second day in the hotel, there were bed bugs in the suite.

"There were bugs crawling up the wall beside the toilet and the manager came up. They had to clean all of our bags and clothing and move us to another suite. Then they gave us 70,000 Sheraton points and Monique and I spent a week in a hotel in Paris for free," Denny says with a laugh. "It was great. Now I just look for bed bugs wherever I go."

BRAD MEHLDAU

One of the most joyous jobs post-sobriety that Seiwell had was with Brad Mehldau.

"Before I met Brad Mehldau, (bassist) Charlie Haden told me, 'You're going to meet this guy soon; he's going to call you. His name is Brad Mehldau and he's probably the most talented guy to come along in the last 50 years.' Charlie might have had a hand in it."

Sometime in the late '90s Brad Mehldau's management approached Seiwell as he was looking to form a trio to perform dates on the West Coast. They set up an audition for Denny and several bass players, and Mehldau and Denny hit it off musically. Darek Oles (Oleszkiewicz) became the bassist to round out the trio.

"I was on pins and needles every gig I played with Brad because the music was so intense and complicated. It would be a lot of odd times and odd phrases; you really had to know the music inside out. I would be asked to solo almost on each tune. It was very intense. Here I was soloing in odd times. It was very challenging," Seiwell admits. "I dug Brad."

They did some gigs, and then Mehldau's career took off and the label began to fly his trio in from New York and Spain. Before he knew it, Seiwell found himself out of the picture altogether.

"I loved the time together with him and we remain friends to this day. He lives in Amsterdam now, married with a family and we stay in touch."

THEY'RE GONNA PUT ME IN THE MOVIES

In 2002 Denny was invited to his friend Charlie Sheen's wedding to Denise Richards. At the table was Sheen's father, mother and brother Emilio Estevez.

"Charlie said to Emilio, 'This guy Denny is a drummer, and he might be able to help you with that movie you're going to do.' We talked for a little bit, and he said, 'I'm writing this movie and there are a couple of scenes where I have to look like I'm playing the drums. Can you help me with that?'"

Estevez kept Seiwell's card for approximately three years, until it was time to film the movie *Bobby* (released in 2006), the fictional movie he had written and was directing, loosely based on Bobby Kennedy, Jr. He was playing the fictional character named Tim Fallon, a drummer in the band at the supposed Ambassador Hotel where Kennedy was giving his victory speech.

"Emilio came over to the house, I sat him down behind my drums and showed him how to hold the sticks to look like he was playing," Denny recalls. "He

Demi Moore as the lounge singer and Denny as the bandleader in a scene from the film *Bobby*, circa 2005. (Photo by Denny Seiwell from dailies he was sent.)

didn't have to play, he just had to look like he was playing; it was pre-recorded music."

Denny gave him a set of electronic drums he had in the house so he could practice at home and the filming began at the Ambassador Hotel, which Seiwell says shut down after some shooting had begun.

"Emilio said he needed some help with the music, which was 1968 big band period music, so I called Dell Hake to help me write some arrangements. One of the songs had to be 'Louie Louie,' and we wrote a couple of others. We went into Capitol Studios with some of the great big band session guys in town and imported these cues for the movie, and Demi Moore was invited down. She sat in the control room, and she got real nervous about getting out there in front of a microphone in front of all these people. She had never sung in public before. I said, 'Don't worry about that. I'll find a nice quiet little place to record your vocals.' She said, 'Oh, that's nice.' I found this studio that was a one-bedroom upstairs apartment in a funky neighborhood in Hollywood. The engineer there had recorded the music with Reese Witherspoon for the *Walk the Line* movie, which was her singing debut, so I thought it might be a good place for Demi. It was just a little one-bedroom apartment. The living room had a piano and a couch, and the bedroom was the control room, and it had all his recording gear. I met Demi there and she walked in and said, 'Is this it?' and I said, 'Yep, this is it.' I told her what had been done there, and she said, 'Oh, that's good.' She plopped down on the couch, I stuck a microphone in front of her face and she sang and went home. That was it—just me, her and the engineer. It was really sweet."

Seiwell had it on tape and he got a call from the production company saying they were going to film it. They filmed the scene at the Canyon Club, dressing the room to look identical to the Ambassador Hotel as it appeared that night. Denny called a bunch of his musician friends to be on-camera in the band, and they were all—including Denny—put in tuxedos and had their hair slicked back.

"When they heard my voice, they said, 'This guy has a great voice; we gotta give him some lines.' Before you know it, I've got a scene with Demi and Emilio who I announce: 'Now, ladies and gentlemen, Virginia Fallon…' I introduced her to the stage. She had a big mink shawl, and I took it off of her."

Earlier at a rehearsal before the show, Denny the bandleader, ushered Estevez, who played Tim Fallon, Virginia Fallon's husband/manager, to the drums with some banter between them and then directed the band while Tim played with the big band. What began as Seiwell prepping the actor on drums, turned into arranging some music, recording Demi Moore, "sidelining" in the on-camera big band that he had to put together and ending up with a speaking scene and credit in the film!

DREAMS COME TRUE

Seiwell had always wanted to play with an organ trio after playing with the Lou Bennett Trio in his Navy days at a club in Barcelona, so he put together a trio with Joe Bagg on Hammond organ and John Chiodini on guitar. "Pretty soon we found some interesting songs—Brazilian, jazz, some kinda funky stuff—and then John said, 'Why don't we do some McCartney songs that you were in on the original recordings, because you're well known for that and maybe we can get a record deal.' So I went out and bought some microphones and stands and wires and we turned that little room into a recording studio. The drums were in one corner and the other corner was a desk that the engineer and producer sat at. The guitar and the organ were in the other two corners. They all went directly into the computer, so we had really good sound sources, and I had really good mics for the drums. I asked Jamie Seyberth, a friend of mine who is actually a distant cousin, who was a hot engineer I had worked with in the studio a couple of times, to come over and help me put it together. I got Pro Tools, we set up the mics and got everything plugged in and gave it the test. Every time we got together, we'd record three or four songs in a couple of hours, and we got really good live sounding takes."

Seiwell says everything just gelled perfectly, organically. One day Chiodini commented that they were making such a nice record with no "suits" around; no record company personnel hanging around. "It's almost as if we're doing it with reckless abandon," he said.

The Denny Seiwell Trio performing at Alva's Showroom in San Pedro, CA, circa 2015. (Photo by Monique Seiwell)

That was it! That became the title of the album: *Reckless Abandon.* There were five McCartney songs included in the great menu of jazz, samba, and funk. Seyberth mixed the record, and Denny's old buddy Jerry Peterson mastered it in the lab at his house. Denny contacted McCartney's office to get licensing on the versions of his material, and he asked photographer Alex Solca to take the cover art. Solca got very creative and asked him to walk around the pool with his cymbal. Denny laid the cymbal down between the pool and the jacuzzi, Denny put the cup of espresso that Monique brought for him on top of the cymbal and voila! The perfect shot!

"The record was done, and we sold it on my website," Denny says of the album, released in 2011. "I was asked to perform at the Beatlefests, and I would sit at the desks and sign my CDs. I would print up pictures of the early days with the band, and I would sell pictures and CDs. I would come home with thousands of dollars. So, it actually made money doing it all myself. That lasted quite a while. I paid the guys every time they came over to the house and when we did gigs, I just gave them the money; I didn't take hardly anything for myself. I was just so appreciative of them."

Around that time, another dream came true when Andrew Surmani, Professor of Music at Cal State Northridge, asked Seiwell to speak on his experience with drugs and alcohol. His friend, Dave Black, a fan of Denny's and the V.P. and Editor-in-Chief at Alfred Publishing, attended the talk. After the talk, Black approached Denny and said, "How would you like to write a drum book?" Denny said, "I've always wanted to write a drum book." Black said, "I'd like to help you write it. I work at Alfred Publishing. Let's see what I can do."

They began conferring about it and working on the book—*What Not to Play! A Drummer's Guide to Crafting a Drum Part*—and Seiwell says Black helped him quite a bit. They went into Drum Channel's studio for a couple of days, set up Denny's kit and filmed him playing along to several McCartney tracks, soundtrack scores, big band charts, odd times, and some jazz tracks. The book was released in 2015.

"It was an instructional book on playing to click tracks, playing big band music and lots of different elements," Seiwell says. "I'm very proud of it."

Shortly after that, through the program, Seiwell met a man named Bruce

The filming of Denny's drum book at Drum Channel Studios, Oxnard, CA, 2015. (Photo by Dave Black)

Quarto, who had a record company called Quarto Valley Records. Quarto went to one of the trio gigs because Denny had been helping one of the label artists with his sobriety, and Quarto respected that.

Denny with Michaela Pereira of *Headline News* after promo interview for new album *Boomerang*, 2018. (Photo by Monique Seiwell)

"He really loved the show and asked if we wanted to do a record. He said, 'I don't have any jazz artists on my label. You can be the one and only jazz artist.' We did a record for him called *Boomerang* (2018). The artwork was phenomenal. Alex Solca took the pictures and then we manipulated them into a beautiful cover. And then Bruce spent the extra money to have it made into vinyl as well. He also spent a ton of money to get us PR with Rogers and Cowan. I was doing interviews every day and I was even interviewed by Michaela Pereira for HLN/CNN."

They decided not to saturate *Boomerang* with McCartney songs but only include the one for which Seiwell is perhaps best known: "Live and Let Die." They made a jazz version of the song, which Denny sent to McCartney. McCartney loved it.

Seiwell says Quarto, the president of the company, was very generous to the band. Sadly, when actor Jeff Goldblum offered Bagg a job he couldn't pass up, the trio came to an end, "And then my emphysema set in and live gigs became more difficult, Denny says.

In about 2021, Fernando Perdomo entered the picture, calling Denny out of the blue one day asking him to go up to his studio to put drums on two Wings songs: *Wild Life*'s "Some People Never Know" and *RAM*'s "Too Many People." Perdomo had recorded a version of the songs with some musicians and wanted him to replace the drums he, himself, had played on the tracks. Skeptically, Seiwell told him to send him the demos. Surprisingly, he was impressed at how well done, and he agreed to the project.

"I went to his studio and put drums on those tracks. It was so easy, I have been playing them in my sleep my whole life. I put down the original tracks, he paid me, and I went home. A couple of months later, he sent me a message saying that the album *RAM* was about to celebrate its 50th anniversary and why don't we record the whole album?"

Perdomo went on to explain to him that he worked with so many young musicians who told him how influential that album was for them and how they liked it even better than some of the Beatles material. It was during the Covid pandemic, and Seiwell agreed. He would go to Perdomo's gear-packed garage studio and sit in the drum booth while Perdomo sat in his control room.

"I think one day we did drums to eight songs," Denny says. "It had to be perfect, or it wouldn't work, and it couldn't be done to a click track because the original wasn't done to a click track. We were doing it and had to come up with a method. So, Fernando played the CD, and I played along with it. We would get the drum track, then do the bass track, then the guitar track and build it out from there. He asked me to help him produce it, and I said yes. We wanted to get it right. He had all these people who wanted to sing and play on it, so we looked for the spirit of the original album. When we found the voice that was right for the part, we tried to make it as close to the original as possible. When we got done with it, it was never more than me and him in the studio. He had a guy send in a part from Amsterdam; there were close to 100 musicians on the album," Denny says.

Some of those musicians and highlights included Marvin Stamm, the original flugelhorn player on "Uncle Albert", and Dave Spinozza, who played the same guitar he played on "Another Day" in 1971. Seiwell used the same snare drum—the one he got from his father—and the little crash cymbal he took from the Navy that he used on the original recording of *RAM*.

When they set out to make the album—*Ram On – The 50th Anniversary Tribute to Paul & Linda McCartney's Ram*—Seiwell called McCartney and told him that there were a lot of young musicians who were aware that *RAM* was coming up on its 50th anniversary and he and his friend Fernando were going to oversee a bunch of younger players who wanted to honor the music. McCartney told him to go ahead and have fun with it. It was great to have his blessing. They applied for all the proper licensing and went through all the necessary red tape. Perdomo had a deal with Cherry Red Records in the U.K., whom they believed would do a great job with their final product, but it turned out to be a disappointment. It went to #7 on Amazon, but Seiwell says the company poorly mishandled the distribution of the album despite all the press they did and the excellent product they turned out. He says they massively dropped the ball. A year later, they released it on double album vinyl, and Denny says he gets an invoice from the label once in a while about how much money they still owe them. After the release in 2021, Seiwell performed the album with about 18 musicians at L.A.'s Troubadour to a sold-out crowd.

Denny continues to work on projects, most recently producing and playing on a record called *The Better Side of Me* for John MacAndrew, his friend of 30 years. Denny says he's very proud of the finished product, which he describes as Americana, a combination of many different genres. Upon completion he played it for his friend Bruce Quarto, who agreed to release it on Quarto Valley Records in May 2025.

OLD FRIENDS

In 2024 McCartney invited the Seiwells down to Henson Studios to hear some tracks he was working on with producer Andrew Watt. When they arrived, it was just Denny and Monique with McCartney and Watt, and McCartney played them a couple of the songs. "Paul played all the drum parts. In fact, Paul played all the instruments, which he does brilliantly," Denny says.

"I teased him and said, 'Ya know, I still do sessions. You could use a real drummer on this stuff. I'd even come down and just do a demo track for you, so you'd have a demo track to work with.' And he said, 'You know, that's not a bad idea.' It was really warm and a very receptive mood. The first track was beautiful, but the second track was a very sentimental kind of nostalgic track. Andrew and the engineer were over at the center of the board and Paul

Paul invited Denny and Monique down to Hensen Studios to hear some of his latest work at the end of 2024. (Photo by Keith Smith)

and Niq and I were over at the other side of the board. Paul is leaning on the board and Niq and I are sitting on some chairs and we're listening to this song that is really beautiful; it's one of his masterpieces. He looks over at Niq and she has tears in her eyes, and then he looks at me and I start welling up and then he leans in and the three of us have a big group hug, and he's got tears in his eyes. Andrew, the producer, was freaking out. It felt like Linda was there—Paul had some things to say about how we had so much history together and so many memories. It was just one of those moments."

When Denny and Monique left that day, nothing was said about getting together again, but it wasn't long after that Denny heard the band was rehearsing in town for their tour. He reached out to Paul asking if there'd be a good day to come say hello.

"He responded and said, 'Let me get back to you and let you know what day is good.' And he did a few days later and he said, 'Why don't you come up next Wednesday at about 2:00.' When we got there, they were sitting outside having a little lunch. I guess they had started in the morning. They sat down and before they knew it, Denny and Paul began exchanging stories about the past and the early days with Wings. They had the band riveted.

"One of us mentioned that Denny Laine was gone, and I said, 'Yeah, it's just you and I left from the original band,'' Seiwell recounts.

Lunch ended and when they went back inside, Denny gravitated toward Abe Laboriel's drums. Laboriel said, "Check out my new kit."

"I wanted to see what they sounded like because they're all metal," Denny says. "So, I went up on the stage and sat down and started tapping around. Paul heard me tapping around and strapped on a bass and came over in front of me and started jamming. And there it was—the magic. It never left. When the two of us played together, there was a magic that happened. That wasn't just in my mind—it was obvious. The looks we exchanged in that moment said it all. The band chimed in, and we grooved a little bit and when that was done, he said, 'As long as we're here, how about playing 'Live and Let Die?' He put his bass down, went over to the piano and kicked it off."

With Denny already seated at the drums, and the band already ready with their instruments, everyone launched into the landmark achievement. Monique whipped out her phone and filmed the historic occurence. It felt like a full circle moment for Denny. He had always mourned the feeling that he would never get to play with Paul again, and at this moment he got to recapture the joy of that blessing.

"The smile on my face and the smile on his face… said it all."

MCCARTNEY'S MEMORIES

Paul: There were a bunch of drummers in New York who auditioned (to do the album). They were all good, but Denny stood out for his drumming and his personality.

Q: What was it about his drumming?

A: He has a very positive style, and he was flexible. My songs aren't always in one vein, so I wanted to try him on the straight rock 'n' roll stuff and then on some more ballady stuff, then something more unusual. There's an old jazz tune called "Caravan" I had him play.

Q: Weren't you just asking him to play beats?

A: I think I said what kind of beats I would like him to do, and as I recall I would tell him something to give him an idea of what area I was looking for. The test piece was really "Caravan" because it starts off with this (sings the intro) and you have to be good to just swing into that.

Q: So, his jazz roots might have gotten him the job?

A: Yes, I think so; the fact that he was able to incorporate that into his playing. Something like that is jazz, but I don't think of it as jazz, I just think of it as a different tempo. If you talk jazz to some people, they may think of a lot of improvisation, but I was thinking more of jazz standards, of which "Caravan" is. It's a particular kind of beat; it swings a little. He was really good at that, he was really good at the slow stuff, he was really good at the straightforward rock 'n' roll, so that's what I mean when I say he was flexible. He could do anything I asked him to do.

Q: What stands out to you about him on *RAM*?

A: I think he contributed to the overall flavor of it. Things like "Uncle Albert," that goes through changes. At first it was the ballad thing I was looking for—just a nice sensitive accompaniment opening. Then it starts going into that (section—McCartney starts singing the upbeat horn part) different beat and to know the changes between these beats and to be comfortable going from a slow thing to a slightly midtempo thing, he was very good at that.

Something like "Smile Away" is more of a straight shuffle, rock 'n' roll beat, blues beat. He was really at home with that, too. Out of all the guys I saw who I asked to do pretty much the same things I asked Denny to do, I thought he was the one who handled it best.

On top of that, as I say, his personality is quite breezy.

Q: Breezy?!

A: (laughs) Breezy! C'mon! He's a fun guy. So that's always important because you're going to have to spend time together, so to have him be fun and amusing and breezy even, was a big plus.

Q: Any other tracks from *RAM* stick out?

A: The track that got away was "Rode All Night," which was just a crazy rocker. We had been to lunch, and we came back into the studio and I just launched into this crazy thing and Denny picked up on it and we were rocking away and captured the spontaneity and spirit, and at the end, I said, "How did that turn out?" to the engineer. And he said, "Oh, you wanted me to record it?" And we go, "Um, yeah, we did. But seeing as you didn't get it, we'll do it again." Of course, the second time is never quite as good. It's still good, but it's never got the energy of the first thing. So, I think that was a big stand-out moment for me; the fact that I launched into it without any warning at all and Denny just came right along with me. That was a good session, except that the engineer forgot to record it.

Q: After *RAM,* when you decided to start a band, that was huge. You had just come from the biggest band in the world and here you were about to start a new band. What were you looking for in the members? This was a huge commitment and what were you comfortable enough with Denny Seiwell to ask him into a long-term band situation?

Another memorable reunion between Denny and Paul at Amoeba Records in 2007. (Photo by Monique Seiwell)

A: It's a lot to do with musicality. You're looking for someone to be able to cover anything you can write and you're also looking for someone who is able to be a band-type person, to sort of roll with the punches. Denny seemed to be up for the challenge. But you're looking for musicality, basically, and for someone who is going to fit with the kind of music you are going to write.

In my case, I didn't know what kind of music I was going to write. I knew it had to be a sound that was different from the sound that the Beatles had. I could have taken an easy route, which would have been to sort of copy the Beatles and stamp out Beatle replicas, but I didn't think that was a good idea. The other thing that I thought, really, was seeing that the Beatles had started at square one—some kids that just knew each other—the secret about it was we grew together, and we were able to feel each other's moods and feelings and thoughts. That was one of the things that was quite a tough decision; if I'm going to go out and do it like the Beatles did it, that means we go and we play little clubs, we don't try to start out at the big stadiums, big arenas. We have to go out and try to find ourselves in the little spots. That meant it was going to be difficult; it was not the easy route, that's for sure. It meant also that any mistakes we were going to make, and with any new band, mistakes are inevitable, and were going to have to be played out in public. People knew who I was, so the first thing they were going to say was, "You're not as good as the Beatles." So we knew we had to suffer those slings and arrows. And we did. It means that it was quite hard going; it was not easy. But we had the spirit. We had this camaraderie which, for me, was an important thing.

Q: Back then it was not Paul McCartney and Wings; it was just Wings. You really intended it to be a real band.

A: Right. Absolutely. It hadn't been Paul McCartney and the Beatles, so I thought if I used the same sort of road map, it shouldn't be Paul McCartney and Wings. It should just be Wings. Many promoters wanted to use my name and have it be Paul McCartney and Wings; they wanted me to do Beatles material, which would have made things easier because it would have meant that we were always playing stuff that people were familiar with. But because of the way, somehow, I foolishly decided to do it, it made it tougher, but now looking back on it, I think it was exactly the right way to do it because we did grow together, and we did make music that didn't sound like the Beatles.

So by using that method, even though it was kind of a bit bizarre, we found our way.

Q: And bonded and had a real band experience like the University Tour. And you began to trust the band's musical instincts more with time.

A: Yes, that's what happens in a band. You start out saying how you want it, but you're only just giving a loose idea of what you want. Then you've got to let your fellow musicians make suggestions and come up with ways they think would improve the song.

Q: Denny said at some point in the recording process you actually sometimes relied on him in the booth.

A: I think sometimes. I think he would agree it was mainly me making the decisions, but if there was a choice going between this way or that way, I would listen to his opinion and often would take it.

Q: How did the idea for the reggae feel on "Love is Strange" come about on *Wild Life*?

A: Reggae was very much a fashionable music at the time, and Linda and I spent holidays in Jamaica, and we would listen to the local radio RJR all day long. We were steeped in the reggae thing when we came back. We loved the original version of "Love is Strange," so we had this idea to change it into our style with a reggae feel. Again, Denny was very good at adapting to that. I think his part on that was very good.

Q: Of course, the quintessential Denny song is "Live and Let Die."

A: Uh huh.

Q: What was that recording like? Denny tells me that song just flowed out of you.

A: Yes, it came quite easily. I had a guy called Ron Kass who worked with us from Apple, the Beatles label in America. Ron had some friends in London including, I believe, the people who did the Bond films. He asked me one day if I would ever consider doing a Bond title track and I said, "Yeah, definitely!" He put it to them, and they said yes. I got the book and read it, and the next day I wrote the song. Then I played it to the guys and to the Beatles producer, George Martin. It flowed quite nicely. There was a little reggae section in the middle, and again, it was one of those things that went in and out of different tempos. It starts off in a more ballad tempo and then goes into a more uptempo, a sort of rocking thing, then there's the reggae thing and back into the uptempo. These are the kinds of things that Denny understood and could cope with easily. That was great. And then when George Martin put his arrangement on it, that really sewed up the whole package.

It was funny because when we finished it and mixed it, George Martin took it to I believe the Bahamas where they were filming the movie. He had to take a boat to the location, and he had some sort of record player with him, and he played it for Cubby Broccoli and said, "Here, here's your song," and Broccoli was supposed to have famously said, "That's a great demo, when are you going to make the record?" George said, "It *is* the record." It was very different from traditional Bond themes, which had been a little more theatrical, but it worked, and many people still consider it one of the best Bond themes.

Q: Which brings me to a recent time where Denny was at one of your rehearsals and you guys ended up playing "Live and Let Die" together. I know it was a wonderful moment for him. What did it feel like for you?

A: It was great. It was great. It was good for everyone in the band. We had only played it with Abe (Laboriel Jr.), our drummer. He does a great version of it. You could see Denny was kind of itching to have a go, ya know, so I picked that up and said, "Why don't you sit in," and he didn't take much persuading. And I must admit, I think all of us might have thought, "I don't know, he might be a little rusty, he might not know it, he might miss a couple of the cues," but far from it. He played it perfectly and it was great. It was a slightly different feel from how we play it, but it was great. He really enjoyed it, but so did we. It was a big moment for all of us.

Q: Was it like an "old friends" moment?

A: Yeah, it was. I was also very pleased for him, that he pulled it off. He could have crapped out; he could have got it wrong, or oops, or this and that. But it wasn't like that at all. It was great; he did it perfectly and so he was very happy and so were we.

After 51 years, Paul and Denny bring back the magic of the beginnings during Paul's rehearsal for his South American tour, 2025. (Photo by Monique Seiwell)

Q: I know for him it feels really good to have those moments. So many people are gone now…

A: Yeah.

Q: …And I would imagine that it would make you cherish the ones who are still here who have been part of your story.

A: That is absolutely true, really. I remember George Martin saying to me once as he was getting on, I asked him, "How is it, George?" And he said, "The main problem is your friends that you've grown up with start popping off. It's so sad, but it's the reality of life." That is true, so you find yourself, when someone like Denny shows up at rehearsal, you feel very nostalgic and you have great memories of how we worked together. It was lovely; it was a moment to cherish.

* * *

As Seiwell reflects on his life in his early 80s, he muses:

"I was a kid from a middle-class family from a small town in Pennsylvania, born with some sort of musical gift. I knew what my life was going to be at nine years old. I excelled in music in high school, played with the older guys and my life was on track. I wasn't afraid to go outside the boundaries—I brought back a fiance from France, which was not done in my hometown. I was breaking rules. Who knew I was going to play with the most famous man in the world?"

Seiwell uses the analogy of a ship and its rudder to describe what came next: the Best and Worst of Times in his life. He describes his life as a rudderless ship when things fell apart, and he didn't know how to find his way back to his goals. He lost his way.

When he found recovery, he says a rudder righted the ship and found his direction, and looking back now, he has the thankful vantage point of having come through the storm intact with the wisdom to know it could have been otherwise had he made different choices. He reflects on the tough lessons he's weathered with the knowledge that often it takes missteps to lead to successes and those grueling challenges build character. He's grateful to God, grateful for all the support he's had on the journey, and to Monique for sticking it out with the hope his story can help others who might be working through their life challenges.

"Life started slipping through my fingers like a handful of sand," he says. "I felt like I couldn't stop it, and then I found recovery. Recovery stopped it. I am writing this hoping that this story can help someone. Adversity is a good thing if you know how to manage it. I'm writing this not to boast about the people I've worked with or the good fortune I've had; it's what you make of your life. I hope it will help whoever is going through a tough time to believe that there is a way out."

Photo by Jess Ferrara.